LIFE

According to
Monty Dogge

By M.T. Sanders

Happy birthday Judy

Hope you have a great day and enjoy my book

Love from Monty

Monty

Cookie

2QT Limited (Publishing)

First Edition 2021
2QT Limited (Publishing)
www.2qt.co.uk

Cover photo by Helen Overmire
Illustrations by Zoe Saunders
Typesetting by Dale Rennard

Printed in Great Britain by IngramSparks

A CIP catalogue record for this book is
available from the British Library

ISBN 978-1-914083-25-9

Contents

Foreword

Mary Burgess - Founder of The Animal Star Awards

I created the awards in 2016 to give recognition to animals and humans alike for the extraordinary things they do for one another. Monty Dogge was chosen as a winner in 2020 for his fabulous blog. Our judge, along with myself, thought the whole concept was such a fantastic idea and I've now invited Monty's owner Mark to be a category judge in 2021.

Monty, you really are everything that epitomises the awards! The books are such a delight not just for children but all ages. I'm so excited to read this latest edition.

Zoe Saunders - Whimsicolour Art

Connecting with Mark and having the opportunity to Illustrate the Monty picture books was a wonderful stroke of luck for me. I was relatively early on in establishing myself as a professional illustrator at the time, and so it was fabulous to be commissioned to work on such a great series. The stories and characters really inspired me creatively – this wise-cracking Newfoundland dog, Monty, and his crazy friend, Cookie, and the silly Spangles were characters that instantly appealed to me as a dog lover. Not to mention the humour and the rhyming prose, and the gentle way of delivering important messages to young readers. It was an absolutely joyful collection of stories to work on, and I'll always be incredibly proud to have my name on the front cover.

Linda – UK

I have followed Monty over the years. For me, being part of a group with the same sense of the ridiculous has made it so enjoyable and helped through difficult times. That Monty went on to raise such amazing sums for charity and do so much for children in schools is remarkable. He is a very worthy hero, personified in a big cuddly dog. He deserves every accolade for his incredible achievements ... with Dad's help, of course!

Jackie – UK

Monty, you are the best! You've done so much for charities and awareness for different campaigns. Your books are wonderful, and your family are fantastic and have helped me smile when I was down. As you know my partner has early-onset Alzheimer's and he loves me to read your books and posts on Facebook. Thank you so much for all you do, Monty and family.

Debra – UK

I have followed Monty since he first appeared on Facebook, and he is a canine hero. His antics never fail to bring a smile to my face, and his words have entered my everyday life. I have two 'Snack Russell terrors' and our vet will forever more be known as 'the vetandhairyman'. Monty is a legend!

David – UK

Don't know where to start. Monty, I started following your daily blog years ago. Made me smile every time I read your exploits. Now, with your books, your school visits, *your work with Ocean Revival and the poppy selling, you're well overdue recognition. I'm proud to have you as a friend on social media.*

Karen – UK

My message to you is very simple: 'You bring sunshine to my life everyday with your antics, and your family put so much work into charities.' Thank you.

Sarah – UK

Sometimes we just need a hero in our lives. Most heroes come with two legs but mine comes with four paws and a wet nose. For all the good you have done for making people happy, Monty, you are my hero.

Lyn – UK

I remember meeting both you and Monty at a big rabbit show – think it may have been in Doncaster. Monty made a big impression as I used to have a St Bernard, and he was a gentle giant too. Sending lots of love to you and your family.

Nick – UK

I've considered Monty as my hero for a good few years now. I've always admired the work he does, particularly for military veterans. Who's that bloke who hangs around with him all the time, though? What does he do?

I fell in love with the Newfoundland breed. They genuinely care and want to help. Our Newfy, Ted, will come and tell you if something is different, or odd , or something has fallen over, or another of our dogs has been sick or something.

Monty's first book nailed the Newfoundland personality so accurately and so beautifully that it inspired me to write a song about him. I'm lucky enough to have met him a couple of times, too.

The money raised for charities online in his name is quite amazing. WE did that, and it was Monty that brought us all together! What a guy.

Jackie – UK

You truly deserve a medal, Monty. You are such a gentle giant. I always love your posts and the antics you get up to ... you bring light, love and laughter to so many. Your books are a delight too Much love to you all and wishing you good luck

Sandra – UK

I first met Monty eight years ago as we also live in Wigan and had a 'Pandacow'. When he was promoting the poppy appeal, we would walk to Sainsbury's just to see him and buy poppies. He always had a crowd around the table – I mean, how could you miss a Newfie?!

Then came the books. They are so relatable that my nieces and nephews loved them, and so did I. When we went out with Stormy, our Landseer Newf, so many children would stop us asking was she Monty because he had been to their school reading books. I would explain that she was his stand-in or stunt double.

Monty has been patiently working for charities most of his life and even going to visit the elderly. So proud of you.

Sally - UK

I remember Monty's Facebook status updates telling us all about his antics – they really made my day. He has invented some amazing additions to the dictionary (and if they are not in there yet, they should be) – Snack Russell, Slobbernosserus, vetandhairyman. His poetry is so good he should be the next Poet Laureate. He's also raised a ton of money for charity. He's an all-round good boy and inspiration to Newfydoofs everywhere.

Jan - UK

You bring happiness to a lot of people, and it was a pleasure to meet you. x

Donna - UK

I absolutely love following Monty and the gang! The stories, funny comments and witty anecdotes are a real treat and bring a lot of laughter! He is loved by so many and works tirelessly in support of others. He truly deserves some recognition for all that he does – fundraising, storytelling, school and nursing home visits, and keeping us hoomans entertained with his home life! Well done, Monty! You are a true superstar! xx

Michael - UK

Monty has brightened my life many times over with his offbeat views of life through the eyes of a Newfie. Well done!!!

Christine - UK

Monty ––not just a dog. There is a story that God ran out of names for all the animals so when it came to the dog, *he reversed the initials of His name. Monty brings so much to so many.*

Sylvia - UK

As former treasurer of East Anglian Working Newfoundlands, your books have been raffle prizes at a yearly event we hold and are very popular. My grandchildren learnt to read with them, too!! X

Helen - UK

Monty always brings a smile to my face, especially in these uncertain times when we can't meet up with loved ones. x

Rachel - USA

I have followed Monty since the beginning. The training videos were hilarious! He wrote a beautiful poem for me that touched my heart when I hit a low point with my Newfoundland rescue... He's a beautiful dog with hilarious and kind 'staff' people'.

Dee - UK

Likewise, we have followed Monty and his antics, plus his hoomans, from the beginning!

Owning Newfies too, we could relate to everything he did! Our last Newfy (Gussyboy) was, I always felt, Monty's twin even though he was a brother from a different mother!

We love all the poems that the poet Newfiette has written, especially the Christmas ones which involved Monty helping pull Father Christmas's sleigh. He travelled all the way to Windsurf to collect Gussyboy so that he could help, too! It was so touching and we will never forget that.

Vivian - UK

Monty, darling, sending all the spangley lubs in the world. A pleasure to hold the much sought after and cherished appointment as personal bib maker to Your Newfieness. Love Aunty Viv, Miss Maisalump and The Fergutron.

Paul - Alaska, USA

Dear Agent, Monty is 'Da Bomb'. All of his antics, and especially the stories of what happens on walkies or when falling-down water is involved, have kept us in stitches for years! Get out there people and collect all of his books (you might want to read them, too!) and please make sure he gets extra treats and bacon... Bacon is good... Signed, all of Yankeedoodleland!

Emma - UK

I stumbled on Monty Dogge's group purely by accident on Facebook. Let's just say it involved a road and number twos!!! I've followed ever since and been entertained with all of the stories he has to tell. I honestly cannot wait for the book to be released. Hopefully I'm on the pre-order list.

Joan - UK

Monty is unique! Charismatic. Fashionista. Fundraiser extraordinaire. Kind. Brave. Can't wait to read the new book.

Christina - UK

It's been wonderful and I feel very privileged to be involved in a small way in Monty's journey, from talking with Mark about the first-ever book to making poppies and troubleshooting on teams!! To see how Monty has touched so many lives is an incredible testament to the hard work and dedication of his hoomans. He's not only raised thousands for charities but awareness around so many issues, both big and small. Here's to the next chapter.

Jenny - UK

I'd just like to say that I've followed Monty's journey right from the start, as Ronnii was his brother. Sadly, Ronnii went to the Rainbow Bridge with cancer two years ago but watching Monts is like having Ron back again. The Christmas book, where they came from Rainbow Bridge to help Santa made me cry, as I knew that Ron was there helping. Keep up the good work. I have all your books, and will buy all those to come. xxx

Mona - UK

I love Newfies I don't have a dog myself but two Newfie nieces. I am always looking forward to Monty's latest thoughts and ideas ... makes my day!

Consuelo - Colorado USA

Oh dear, Monty Dogge, when the tweenster was just a mini-hooman she was introduced to the famous Pandacow and his lovely home of Wigwam! We love everything about Mighty Monty, every story, every thought, and all the wonderful things he and Cookie and his hoomans do for good causes (and the Spangles are quite silly, too)! We have introduced his stories with classes of very-mini mini-hoomans here in the mountains of Yankeedoodleland and have spread love and awareness of all things Monty. We love you, Monty! From Jaxon and Consuelo

Jennifer – Texas USA

Monty, Cookie, the Spangles and their hoomans have a way of crawling into your heart, putting a smile on your face and making every day better. I have laughed, I have cried, and then laughed again. Monty and all of his crew are so special, and do more to make this world a better place than they realize. I just wish I wasn't so far away in Yankeedoodleland. Giving Monty a snuggle followed by a treat or two would be amazing. Just to say thank you for all of the smiles, laughter and happiness you have blessed us with.

Cathy – UK

My grandson loves your books, and my daughter read them to her foster children. My Tripaw Jack and I met you both at Crufts. It was lovely to watch you both with the children.

Pip – UK

We have been following from the beginning, with an initial connection through the Spangles. Then you came within a mile of our home when you did the swimming and rescue training at Watermead. The books have bought us great happiness, but they have also been a way of spreading the word to our 'adoptive' nephews and nieces and friend's children.

Ultimately, our admiration is for your kindness and support to various charities, especially when my friend's daughter was dying and you took some of your precious time to drive over a hundred miles each way to meet with the family and spend time with them at the most difficult time of their lives. Isla loved that afternoon, as did the rest of the family.

Thank you is too simple, but nevertheless totally heartfelt.

Narelle - Australia

We have followed from your very early days, Monty, and to be able watch your journey over the years has been such a treat for us Aussies from Upsidedown Land, and something we'll always treasure! We have eagerly awaited the pigeon's delivery of your book each time and have thoroughly enjoyed every story! Your Christmas poems have been fabulous and your imagination is spectacular, even though I think sometimes Dad tries to claim the fame for that... 😜 We'll let him keep believing it, hey Mont? 😊 Seriously though, we are so glad that you, Cookie, Dad, Pipsqueak and the rest of the fabulous crew that makes up the Wigwam Gang came into our lives. You do your best to make people laugh, smile, care about the planet and for all of the people around us so we are honoured to be able to share your life with you and to call you our friends!

Ginny - UK

Just has been such a delight to read of Monty's adventures over the years and see those adventures finally put into print. The joy and humour that you've brought to so many is truly wonderful, not forgetting your amazing fundraising. My hero Monty – thank you.

Patty – Baltimore USA

Oh my, not even sure where to start!!!

By his actions, words and stories, Monty inspired me to reach out and help others! So much so that I did a fundraiser here in Yankeedoodleland and raised enough money to share his story and books with over 200 children!!! He's opened my eyes to the amazing philanthropic work dogs/animals do in the world and I am forever grateful!

Oh, and I LOVE his family!!!

Introduction

Early in 2021, we were delighted to be awarded first place in the prestigious Animal Star Awards Best Pet Blogger category. When I say 'we', it's because for me personally this award was a wonderful recognition of Monty and the effect he has had on so many people over the years.

Not only has he raised thousands of pounds for charity and toured more than a hundred schools with his stories, he has been a massive inspiration for me. In 2010, following a head injury suffered in an accident at work which left me with cognitive issues, I was forced to take early retirement. My mental state was very poor, I suffered a series of complications from the injury and I was severely depressed.

In 2011 we took the decision to welcome a new addition to the family and Monty joined Molly, Bailey and Poppy, our three Cocker Spaniels. I had always wanted a Newfoundland and had watched videos of their amazing water-rescue feats. The family felt it might be the boost I needed to support me on the road to recovery.

I don't want to spoil the book, but the water-rescue part never really went as expected. However, Monty certainly helped me. Suddenly my head was full of stories. Monty's huge personality and zest for life made me want to try and express how he saw the world.

I'd always loved writing stories and poems and I'd had a couple of poems published in my teens, but earning an honest living was the priority. It wasn't until Monty arrived that I picked up my pen again – or rather my keyboard.

What started with a Facebook page of Monty stories ended up with seven published children's books and this year was topped off with our Animal Star award, of which I am very proud.

Monty has been an inspiration to me. He has helped me get through the worst part of my life, and because of that he has been the best part of my life. I can never express how much I owe him. I hope you enjoy his story.

Monty and Mark with the Animal Star Award

CHAPTER 1
Home

March 2011

Monty, our first Newfoundland came to live with us in March 2011 as a seven-week-old puppy. We already had three Cocker Spaniels in what was a 'busy' household that also consisted of four adults and three children.

What followed changed our lives as we attempted to get to grips with living with a puppy that was growing faster than a politician's expenses' claim.

Monty on his journey to his new home

His new family. The spangles L to R Molly, Poppy, Bailey

He made us laugh, cry and most days question our sanity, but above all he always entertained. This is his story ... in his own words.

This is life according to Monty Dogge...

When I were a pup, I don't remember too much,
Then two hoomans came for a look and a touch.
They were new ones to me, never seen these before,
And me mum Newfydoofed them as they came through the door.

They seemed to be shocked and I thought they might run
But they seemed to enjoy it, me new dad and mum.
Though I didn't know it, they had come to see me
And the rest, as they say, is Monty Dogge history.

At first, they seemed unsure – would it be me or another?
They kept picking us up, me and me brother.
Then all of a sudden me feet stayed off the floor
And we all started heading towards the front door.

We got in a car, but I was a baby,
And I got pretty scared about where they would take me.
Then, all of a sudden, things began to whizz past –
I clung on to me new mum, 'cos the world moved so fast.

At last we arrived at the place they called home,
And I'm not scared to say that I felt all alone.
I shouldn't have worried 'cos when I walked in
There were dangly-eared doglets – and my what a din!

I'd never seen ears that hooge or so flappy,
And they ran round in circles and seemed really happy.
That changed when I went to say my hellos –
They growled and walked off, didn't want to know!

Though these strange doglets were the same size as me,
We looked very different; it was clear, you could see.
I was worried 'cos my ears, though big, didn't dangle,
But Dad said, 'Don't worry, Monts, these are Cockeyed
Spangles.'

Molly was grumpy; she'd seen this before.
She used to be the only one, but not any more.
Then came Poppy, she was orange and white,
And her breath smelt real bad like she'd been eating... (not very
nice stuff).

Bailey was the youngest, not much older than me,
And that was me new housemates – the mad Wigwam Three.
They joined in together and picked on me a lot
So when I grew big, they deserved what they got!

If they annoyed me I just sat on their heads,
And I tried to eat their food after I had been fed.
But the best thing was stealing toy they liked best
And watching as they jumped and reached only me chest.

Those days seem a way off, a long time ago,
But we can't stay as babies; we all have to grow.
As I get older, I know I've grown up
But I still like to remember when I were a pup.

Mighty Monty   *It's all a bit too much*

5th April 2011

That was a really long journey, but we've arrived at my new home now. I should be happy and excited, but all I feel like is looking at the insides of me eyelids.

Sleeping is great I could do it all dazzzzzzzzzzzzzzzzzzzz...

I'm learning everyone's names now. There is hooman dad, who sometimes gets called Homer. Hooman mum is just Mum – I don't fink anyone is brave enough to call her anything else. They have grown-up children, and the one who lives with us is Poobag ... well, that's what Dad calls her: 'Er, quick, Poobag. Just over here, Poobag.'

I know it's a funny name but she seems to like it OK. Poobag also has mini-hoomans... I know, it's complicalated, ain't it? Hoomans everywhere in our house. Try to keep up though, please.

6th April 2011

My strange doglet brothers and sisters are definitely getting smaller every day. Their ears don't seem to be shrinking though, and they're much too big for their heads.

Been paddling in me water bowl, chewing Mum's Crocs and hanging off Poppy's ears. It's time for a zzzzzzzzzzzzzzzzzzzzzzzz...

Poppy's ears are fun

Look how long I am Bailey

7th April 2011

Today I'm off to Pets-All-You-Can-Eat-Before-You-Get-Told-Off. The hoomans call it summat different, but there is food everywhere and I can't help myself. After all, I'm a growing pupster and I need me Newfydoof fuel.

14th April 2011

My first day at water training tomorrow. I'm hoping to have a licckle paddle and maybe a trip in the boat. Weee-heee, can't wait. I've been told that one day I'll be a water-rescue dog and a great swimmer. I don't know what any of that means, but hopefully I can eat it.

22nd April 2011

I fink the hoomans may have ideas about making me a show dog, cos tonight I'm off to summat called 'ringdaft'. It learns me how to walk proper in front of the judge. Or maybe I'm going to court. Surely I haven't been that norty, have I?

I came second in the puppy walk tonight. I think I like sitting down too much. Maybe swimming is my thing – or maybe not. Maybe I don't have a thing.

We thought at one point that Monty might make a good show dog, but Monty had other ideas. Then we had hopes of him as a rescue dog. We joined a water training group for Newfoundlands but the rest was down to him, so Dog knows how that would go.

27th April 2011

I went to a hooge lake wiv lots of other Newfydoofs and hoomans. I went in the water and had a bit of a paddle. Everyone was saying I'm a natural, but I've seen now what they make the big doglets do – pulling hoomans along in the water! Have you seen the size of Dad? He ain't no lightweight so I don't fancy that at all. Maybe I need to stop being a 'natural'.

A first swim

That's a nice toy

Do I have to rescue you Dad?

24th May 2011

The shiphead game. Mum and Dad have this fun game they play when we walk in the woods. To teach me to stay close, they hide behind a tree when I'm not looking and then, when I run to find them, they jump out and scare me.

Today I thought I'd play a game too, so when they hid I found a big pile of poo and rolled in it. When I ran, Dad jumped out and went 'BOO!' and went to tickle me. Then he went 'Aaaargggh' and they both pulled a funny face. It was great fun, and all the way back they called me 'shiphead'. I like this shiphead game, it's sooo fun.

25th May 2011

Molly and Bailey are off to get a haircut today. Poppy says that if I jump up and get the treat box down while they're out, she'll help me eat them.

26th May 2011

I managed to poo right outside the conservytree door, which sent Mum and Dad into a panic. While they tried to stop the other dogs treading in it and cleaned up, I managed to drink Mum's tea. I do like watching the hoomans run around, they're very funny.

27th May 2011

If a tree falls in the forest and nobody is around to hear it, does it make a sound? Is that the same as if I eat something off the table and nobody sees me? Does that mean that I didn't do it? I've heard there's an Irish fella called Phil O'Soffical and he says fings all deep and meaningful, so I fort I'd give it a go.

> Monty was like a people magnet when we took him anywhere. Sometimes this was a good thing and sometimes it wasn't, but usually his mere presence made people smile.

28th May 2011

Just been fussed by a lady who hasn't stroked a dog for forty years since being bitten as a child by a police dog. I got her over it with my Newfydoof power. She couldn't resist.

3rd June 2011

I've had a bad cough. It's summat called Colonel Cough. I don't know who he is but I'm not happy he gave me his cough. Just had a spoon of Manuka honey and some buttercup syrup. Dad said that they must be golden flippin' bees for thirty-four quid. I like these golden bees.

15th June 2011

Feeling a lot better today, no coughing. Thank you, golden bees.

16th June 2011

Mum says I've got the devil in me today. Well, I've been for two poos and there's no sign of him. He must still be in there.

Two against one isn't fair

See how you like it

22nd June 2011

Dad has bought me a ramp to get in and out of the car 'cos he says I'm a big lump. Ha-ha, talk about the teapot calling the saucepan black...

I overheard the hoomans saying that was the end of Auntie Biotic. Poor auntie, wonder what happened to her?

Had a nice trip to Pets-At-All-You-Can-Eat-As-Long-As-You-Are-Quick. Got a new toy and lots of fusses. I love these all-you-can eat buffets. There seems to be some debate about whether this is one or not. I think it is. Debate over.

23rd June 2011

Mum and Dad are stressed out, Poppy has come into season, whatever that means. I don't think it's my fault this time, but we were play fighting last night and now she's bleeding so maybe it was...

24th June 2011

Hooman mum and dad keep saying, 'Jesus, we need a bigger bed.' I wish Jesus would get them one soon. I really struggle to stretch out with them two in there.

Just been out for my little road walk. Dad says I need to be good on my lead. No jumping up at hoomans, no chasing hoomans in moving tins, and no barking at little doglets. You're not really selling these walks to me, Dad.

Bailey was looking fed up so I went and sat next to him. I said, 'Why the long face then?' He didn't get it.

25th June 2011

I think those long dangly ears are a serious design fault. Why Poppy thinks it's attractive to fling wee-smelling ears around beats me.

28th June 2011

Had a bath today. Don't like those stairs much, or the shampoo, or standing still, or towels, or not being able to play with the mini-hoomans bath toys. It's a tough life being me.

> Monty was growing at a phenomenal rate and what was unreachable yesterday suddenly became his today. It was like having a huge hairy toddler that was rapidly growing to the size of an adult.

10-week
Monty

14 weeks.
Catching up

20 Weeks.
Hello shortie

4th July 2011

I've realised that if I stand up on my back legs, I can now serve myself from the kitchen counter. It saves Mum and Dad feeding me. How considerate am I? They are really pleased. They called me a 'big pain in the butt', which is good because before I was only a 'little git'.

Poppy has a funny smell coming from her, it makes Bailey run around panting all day. When I do a funny smell I just get shouted at. Girls – it's not fair.

I hope one day I can rescue hoomans too. I want to drag them gently into shore with my strong jaws and then quietly go through their pockets to see if they have any treats.

Ha-ha, Bailey's in trouble. He peed in the house and blamed it on the Poppy smell. Guess who'll be getting all the fuss today, 'cos I'm a good boy. Na-na-na-na-na.

5th July 2011

Has anyone got the instructions on how to open a Beko fridge door? A diagram would be great, if you have one. There looks like there are some interesting things in there. I'm asking for a friend.

These hoomans are really hard to train and they drive me crazy. Dad says I shouldn't jump up at people. Ok, Dad, maybe you should tell them to stop coming up to me with that funny squeaky voice going, 'OMG, he's beautiful! HELLO, gorgeous! I want one! I want one!' Jeez, what do they think I'm going to do? Have a lie down?

I have never eaten my own poo, chewed pants or socks, don't roll in dead carcasses or run away from my own shadow. I just don't fit in with the other doglets in me family.

> Every day the walks were an adventure, although not always a wonderful adventure. Often it was the kind of adventure you want to end. Soon.

6th July 2011

Training again this morning. Walk nicely on a lead... Check. Ignore the moving people with wheels... Check. Don't eat any schoolchildren. Two out of three ain't bad, is it?

7th July 2011

Typical: I get an owner who doesn't understand gardening. Eating the tops off roses on our walk is called 'Deadheading Dad'.

I was looking forward to meeting the small white dog on my walk today, but the hooman dragged him away and crossed over the road. Then they crossed back behind me. Never mind, when we went further on our walk we saw him again. The strange hooman did exactly the same thing. That dog must have been really vicious. Phew, I'm glad I didn't meet him again.

Why was everyone so surprised when I let myself out? Do you really think door handles are that complicated, hoomans? Still waiting for instructions on the fridge door, though.

OK, I may have bitten off more than I can chew on my walk. I'm partial to some fox poo – we all are, right? But I grabbed a load with a mouthful of grass and couldn't get it down quick enough.

Mum did the, 'What's that in your mouth, Monty?' followed by the hand in me gob and then, 'Bluurgg! What the hell is that? OMG, I feel sick.' Whooops. Bad boy Monty.

8th July 2011

Thought for the day. Friendship is like peeing on yourself: everyone can see it, but only you get the warm feeling that it brings. You're welcome.

11th July 2011

Some people dream of winning the lottery and buying a big house. Some people yearn for fast cars, fine jewellery and expensive holidays. Some people think of this so much, they never think of anything else. Me? I just want my front legs to grow a bit so they are the same length as my back ones. These growth spurts are killing me, man. Copy and paste this on your status if you also want your front legs to be longer.

Come on front legs, catch up.

17th July 2011

Mum and Dad said my dodgy stomach must have been because something I ate disagreed with me. Well, if it didn't want to be eaten it should have said so at the time. It's a bit late now to disagree.

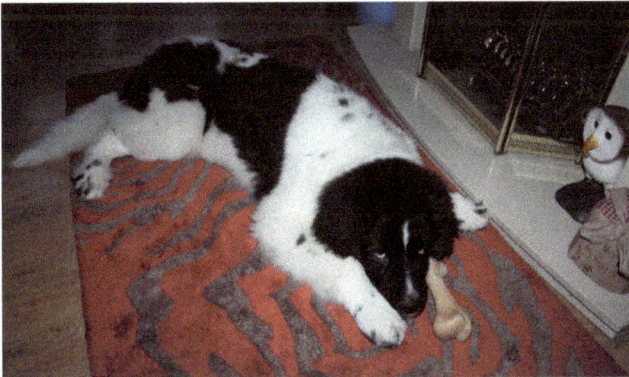

Someone's feeling sorry for themselves

19th July 2011

Am continuing on my quest to understand the two-legged ones. I was just minding my own business and having a quiet number two in the garden when Dad comes running across going, 'It's a firm one! Good boy, Monty.' He was very excited. I think he needs to get out more.

CHAPTER 2
More Holes Needed

I think it's fair to say that Monty was a difficult puppy. He liked eating as much of his surroundings as he could, doing pretty much his own thing and generally being a huge white-and- black hooligan. We decided that what he needed more than anything was lots of socialising and training. Guess who got that job? ... Yep

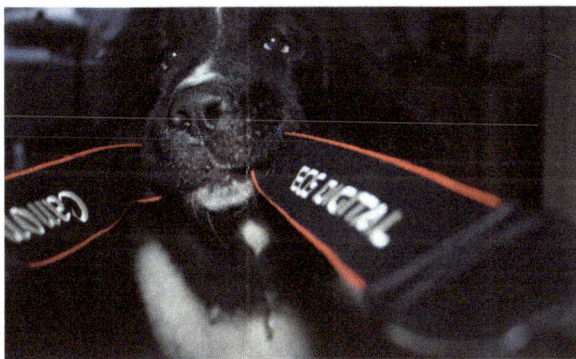

No more pictures. Give it here!

21st July 2011

Now the learning zoos are on holiday, I am going to a busy shopping centre this morning to carry on with my training. Dad said training with mini-hoomans, so they must be the treats, right? Wonder how many I can eat?

24th July 2011

Dad said me and Mum had a snoring competition last night and he couldn't sleep. Guess who won... Congratulations, Mum.

25th July 2011

Dad's improving, but he wants to stop every time he meets other hoomans

I've just been to the shops again. I had a queue to meet me today. Dad says he's going to take up busking and make a fortune. Shame he can't sing or play any musical instruments.

27th July 2011

What shall I do today? Housework? Gardening? Go to work? Nah, probably just have a couple of strolls, eat lots and snooze in the sun. Just remind me again who is the superior species. i

> Monty seemed able to eat or destroy anything and everything. His favourite trick was to chew the garden hose so that it had holes everywhere. I repaired it so many times that eventually the hose was about four-feet long

Just put some extra holes in the hose so now it cools me down with nice sprinkly water. Mum and Dad are not happy. I got told off there's no pleasing these hoomans. I fort they'd love the extra irrigation, but no. It seems they are happy with just the one hole in and one hole out. Boring.

Dad fixed it so I think I'm forgiven now. I've eaten some concrete, chewed the mat and rearranged a piece of skirting board since then, so they don't seem too bothered about the hose anymore.

28th July 2011

Why do you hoomans spend hours writing stuff to each other? Just go and sniff their bum.

31st July 2011

Practised my swimming yesterday. Swam out to the boat and back, swam out to Poobag and back, swam out to my toy and brought it back. Dad says I was brilliant and a very good boy. I'm speechless – I'm not used to being a good boy and it's a strange feeling. Everyone says I can do my 'A' test now. Sounds painful to me.

Monty swims out to the boat.

2nd August 2011

Bakewell Show tomorrow. Lots of bunnies, sheep, horses and other doggies. Will I be a good boy?... Ha-ha two chances ... fat and none.

I didn't do a fing wrong at the show. I can't take the credit though, it was all down to that pesky spoilsport lead and Dad's alertness to mischief... Not fair.

14th August 2011

Nice walk this morning. Bit of a paddle, saw two swans, kept away from those psychos. Met a whirlwind of Spaniels, bit boring 'cos I've got some of them at home. On the way back met Raven the Cavi. He's alright, a pretty cool guy. His sister is pug-ugly though.

16th August 2011

I'm sorry to the man who I jumped on in the woods last night. I'd been playing with two friends and was a bit giddy. Dad says I am a 'bloody lie ability', which must be a good thing, I think. I'm doing some more training now – 'Monty must not jump on people' training. I think it's going to be hard to learn this one.

The man was wiv a group of girl hoomans when he saw me. He started shouting, 'It's a bear, it's a bear,' then he ran off. All of the girls were laffing, so I fort he wanted to play.

I was in front of Dad and I heard him shout, 'Don'ttttttttt Ruuuuuuuun,' but I didn't mind. Running is fun. It was only later, when Dad caught up and I was sitting on the hooman and giving him kisses, that I realised he meant the man shouldn't run, not me. Oops.

> Eventually Monty was ready for his test on the path to becoming a water rescue dog. The question was: was the Newfoundland world ready?

17th August 2011

Time to start packing for my weekend away. I have downloaded a Newfie's guide to passing your 'A' test, as it was recommended to digest the contents before you go. It didn't taste great to be honest, but I think it's pretty well digested.

21st August 2011

Just back from the country called Essecks. Didn't pass my test 'cos Dad messed up, but I had a great time. Met my two sisters, my half-sister and half-brother, and lots of other friends. I thought all the Essecks girl Newfies would be blonde and called Sharon or Tracey, but they weren't. Bit disappointed, really.

> The speed at which Monty was growing certainly caught us out on many occasions. When staying in a chalet, you'd think that closing the door would keep a seven-month-old Newfie in, wouldn't you? Wrong again.

22nd August 2011

You can always tell new Newfie owners. An experienced one would have shut those windows in the licckle house we were stopping in. As they say, though, every schoolboy error is a Newfie's bonus, and I managed to take myself out for a walk. The brown long-eared one could only watch in wonder as I leapt out. I sometimes feel sorry for his midgetness ... but only for a second or two.

It took the hoomans ages to realise I was gone. I had a great time, made lots of new fwends and helped them wiv their food.

Should have closed that window

23rd August 2011

I opened the back door last night by myself. Been looking at it for a while, but last night the hoomans were out in the garden eating Barbie's food so the motivation was there. Got a round of applause. Easily pleased, these two-legged ones.

I knew those Cockeyed Spangles were strange little dogs, but the Poppy one has a new obsession – eating my poo. So now a bloke can't even have a quiet dump without some ginger mop-eared dung beetle waiting for something to drop. Disgusting little creature.

25th August 2011

Just been for a lovely walk in the sun down through the woods and along the canal. Then we went down past the lake and I fancied a bit of a swim, but Dad said that blue-green Al guy was in there. Can someone tell him to get out so I can have a swim, please?

Don't think I'd like to see someone that colour. Dad goes a bit green when he drinks the falling-over water, but not blue and green.

26th August 2011

I thought everyone needs cheering up a bit;

May the sun always shine on your windowpane;
May a rainbow be certain to follow each rain;
May the hand of a friend always be near you;
May a Newfie fill your heart with gladness to cheer you.
May you never tread in poo when you go into the garden.

I did change it a bit ... can you tell? I fink that maybe I could be a poet. Maybe I'll give it a go.

CHAPTER 3
Just Call Me Bisto

It was becoming pretty clear that Monty wasn't all that crazy about swimming. He was very lazy and didn't follow directions well, hardly the qualities of a highly trained rescue dog – or even a badly trained rescue dog, for that matter.

28th August 2011

Failed my test again today. Dad says he's going to rename me Bisto ... something about me being a laughing stock. I know he don't mean it though, 'cos he keeps telling me I'm a good boy and giving me hooman kisses.

The judge said I was eighteen seconds too slow. Eighteen seconds? I do work to Newfydoof time and it's a bit different to hooman time ... I thought they would have known that.

The problem was the hoomans again. Dad went out on the boat and Mum was holding me at the side of the water. They didn't shout to let me go but I knew it was time, so I took Mum along with me into the lake. It's not my fault she was wearing her normal clothes and didn't want to swim. Always complaining, these two-legged ones.

I am always asked what swimming stroke Newfydoofs do. Well, I prefer the doing the doggy piddle – it warms me legs! Ya get me?

Wow I'm tired tonight. Just fancied scratching me ear but couldn't be bothered... It can wait...zzzzzzzzz.

> Monty has always had a bit of a strange relationship with the Spaniels. They gang up on him whenever they get the chance and try desperately to get the better of him. Bailey and Monty are very funny together because it's fair to say Bailey isn't the sharpest, and Monty takes advantage at every opportunity.

30th August 2011

That's it. The Cockeyed Spangles just had a walk in the woods and what did I get? A trip to the wholesalers and garden centre. Whoopy-doo, lucky me. I can see them laughing at me from behind their stupid ears.

That was the most boring bring trip ever. I couldn't even go into the garden centre thingy-wotsit, it was for Guy's dog only. How come he can take his dog in with him? Not fair.

The most exciting thing was doing a poo with no bin for miles, so they had to drive with me elephant droppings stinking the car out for miles. Serve 'em right.

This morning I've been winding Bailey up so he bites me and then I jump on him. I've wrecked the servatree place and trampled Mum and Dad's bed. What can I do now? Maybe a hooge drink of water and then rub me face along the hoomans' legs.

That god person spent so long on Bailey's ears and big eyelashes he forgot to put his brain in. Honestly, if he were any stoopider he'd be a hooman.

Winding Bailey up. Not hard.

31st August 2011

Dad has ordered me a new bib cos he said I am a big slobbery beast. Me? Well, I hope he's ordered himself one as well.

I think there will be some writing on it. I'd quite like 'HI LADIES ... Monty Dogge is in da house'. What do you think?

1st September 2011

To my friends: 'Remember not to frown, for I know someone who is in love with your smile.' Isn't that a nice thought for the day? I'm not very good at smiling but I like it when the hoomans do it because I usually get food or a fuss straight after. Making hoomans smile seems like a good thing to learn.

Just been to the vetandhairyman to get weighed. They said I was thirty-nine keynose. Dad says I'm putting weight on nice and gradually. Personally, I like the idea of putting weight on nice and really, really quickly.

That was a hard walk today. Dad doesn't usually pull that badly. He needs a bit more hooman training, I think.

Just been down the woods playing with a Pattacake terror. Jeez, they can run! Couldn't catch the little devil and then, when I sat down for a breather, I'm sure that was a raspberry he blew in me face. Or was it a kiss? Does that mean he fancies me?

Oh no, I just made a really school-Newf error. Managed to sneak Dad's wallet thingy-wotsit and then sauntered off into the servatree by meself. I was being quiet and I heard him say to Mum, 'Monty's quiet, he must be up to something.' Got me this time, hooman slave, but I'll be back. It was sooo crunchy, too. Mum says it was because of all the moths.

> Apart from the rapid growth in size, Monty's personality was getting bigger. You could see what he was thinking, and most of the time he managed to work everyone out – including us, his hoomans.

4th September 2011

Happy Buffday, Poobag! Now, can you hurry up and take me for a walk? xx. Anyway, time for a cheery celebration song for her.

Happy birthday to you, you look 32.
You have lots of children,
And they're silly like you!

5th September 2011

In my house there are hoomans. Hoomans make a flippin' mess and never do what they're told. If you have hoomans that make your life a misery, repost this, send me some treats in the mail and they will magically disappear.

12th September 2011

It's raining, it's pouring, guess who's been snoring?

Off to Ruff Luck Rescue dog show next weekend. Should be fun. Watch out, all Cockeyed Spangle owners, 'Pretty Boy' Bailey has been curling his eyelashes.

It's my show debut at the Ruff Luck show on Sunday. I think it will be a short career, starting and ending with me humiliating hooman dad which won't be a bad thing.

Bailey, on the other hand, will turn up with his ears freshly ironed, eyelashes curled and wearing his smoking jacket. I can picture him now fluttering his lashes at the judge and going, 'Look at me, I'm a ickle puppy dog wiv big bwown eyes.' You gotta love the pretty boy.

Monty's show debut

Didn't he do well

Pretty Boy Bailey

15th September 2011

Went for a walk last night and some rowdy hoomans were blocking the path with their bikes and wouldn't move. They were a bit lippy with my hoomans, so I showed them how white my teeth were. Hope they managed to get their pants clean.

Shame Bailey wasn't there, he would have slapped the blackguards in the face with his driving glove and challenged them to a duel.

> Monty was strong when out on a walk. Add in stubbornness and an interest in chasing cars and buses to the mix, and it wasn't a great combination. It made us think we needed a little more control.

17th September 2011

Just had another new present … a head collar, whoopy doo. I feel like a flippin' horse with it on. Tell you what, it's coming off the first chance I get. Maybe I should see if I can get the hoomans an iron mask for Xmas and see how they like it.

I can see it coming – they'll be feeding me carrots soon and I'll have a nosebag, won't I?

> Despite the passing of time, Monty was no less destructive. In fact if anything, the bigger he got the more damage he seemed to do.

19th September 2011

Happy Birthday, Bailey, me licckle mate. You're one today. Does that mean you're not a pupster anymore? Just the size of one... Here's a little song for you:

> Happy Birthday to you,
> Where has all that time flew?
> You're a weird Cockeyed Spangle
> How come you've not grew?

20th September 2011

I sort of knocked me dad's coffee all over his lappytop thingy this morning and now it's dead. He's having to borrow Mum's, which he says is as difficult as trying to prise a Newfydoof off a rump steak... He does say some strange things sometimes.

22nd September 2011

That's it, Dad's ordered a new lappytop thingy. He says it's coming out of my ice-cream fund (what ice-cream fund would that be?). I just think he should send this stoopid face-hugger collar back and get a refund. Anyway, what happened to innocent until proved Bailey didn't do it?

28th September 2011

Off to the beach today. It's a tough life. I wouldn't wish this on anyone. I suppose it'll be alright as long as the hoomans behave themselves. Dad said I sulked last time when I had to come off the beach. Ah, is that what throwing yourself on the floor and refusing to move is? I've learnt another new word.

But I want to stay on the beach!

Part of Newfoundland water training is the art of the underwater retrieve. This is where an item must be picked up by the dog from beneath the surface – not one of Monty's strong points.

30th September 2011

Been practising me underwater retrieve today in the paddling pool. I am officially the world champion at blowing bubbles out of my nose... I love it

1st October 2011

Everyone went out today and left me in the kitchen. I wanted to go too, but the door was shut so I fort I'd make a new one.

It was hard work making summat I could fit through wiv just me teefies, so I gave up. Then I got bored and decided to see if they'd left any food in the cooker fingy. It had a big glass door but I managed to open it wiv me paw. It wasn't very well made 'cos I only stepped on it and it broke all over the place and...

I jumped up to check the top to see if there was any food on there, but it started making a hissing noise so I fort I'd best leave it. The hoomans came back then and they was shouting and running around. Dad opened all the windows. It was nice and breezy. I sensed they weren't very happy wiv me again. Not sure, but I don't fink I should have tried to make a new door...

4th October 2011

Doing some more training this morning. I am trying to train Dad not to pull on the lead. I have got to the stage where I make the lead go loose and he makes a silly noise and gives me a piece of chicken... He's coming along nicely.

25th October 2011

Just been for me walk and I was a really good boy, so I slipped my lead when I got back and tried to get back out again, then I attacked the hose and the broom when Dad was trying to clean up. He'd get soooo bored if I was good all day.

> We persevered with the show-dog ambitions – it seemed such a shame to keep those stunning good looks all to ourselves. But we were getting some really strong hints that Monty didn't share our enthusiasm.

26th October 2011

Just got me new show lead and collar today, very nice. It just won't fit over me head. Seems like a basic mistake to me but hey, what do I know? I'm only a dog.

27th October 2011

Going to something called ringdaft again tonight. Poobag says I can be a show dog. Well, as you know I'm a bit of a philosopher and I believe anybody can be anything they want. Except Bailey, he can't be clever. Oh, and Dad – he can't be witty. But apart from that...

Welcome to the world of the show dog. Stood in a line most of the night with dogs I couldn't play with, then ran round in circles past dogs I couldn't play with. Then I had to stand still while a chap ran his hands all over me and not in a fuss-type way. Then he checked to see if I had me boy bits... I do. Did he have to check three times?

Seriously, I worry about hoomans sometimes.

28th October 2011

Made a little friend last night. He was a very cute little dog called a Keysound ... funny name. He was playing 'who can bark the loudest' with me. I won and he got a little bit scared, but I'm looking forward to playing again at ringdaft.

31st October 2011

Got me new show collar. Wow, what can I say? It's like wearing a thong round your neck. Some will know that feeling better than others (you know who you are).

Just can't wait to be bathed, brushed, clipped and sprayed with smelly stuff, then – oh yeah, mincing round in circles. Does life get any better than this? That was doglet sarcasm, if you didn't realise.

1st November 2011

I know it's childish but being able to burp and fart at the same time does make me chuckle. ROFB.

That's Roll On the Floor Barking FYI...Try to keep up, please.

CHAPTER 4
Attack Of The Killer Clothes Airer

Monty has always been obsessed by the other animals in the house, the rabbits, guinea pigs and the chickens. The chickens have never once backed down in front of him; instead, they chase him back into the house where he hides.

2nd November 2011

I swear I didn't know if I stood on top of the wooden run fingy-bobby it would break. I was only trying to get a good look at the licckle bunny wabbit.

I didn't eat it. I love the bunnies. Now, those evil, feathered, clucking things – if I could just get hold of them... Mmm, I feel like chicken tonight.

4th November 2011

I'm new to all this Cwissymouse stuff 'cos I've never seen one before, but this Santa geezer is scaring me a bit. You heard this?

> He sees you when you're sleeping,
> He knows when you're awake,
> He knows if you've been bad or good
> So be good for goodness' sake.

That is creepy. It probably infringes me doglet rights.

> When out with Monty, we were getting used to some of the comments from people we met. The first few times they were even quite funny.

6th November 2011

Had a lovely walk at Rother Valley park today. It took a long time because people kept stopping us and saying 'It's not often you see Saint Bernard' and 'When will he carry some brandy?' and 'Where's his saddle?'... and zzzzzz. Sorry, nodded off there for a second.

One hooman said, 'Look at him, he's a big lad.' I really took offence at that cos Dad has been trying to lose a bit of weight l recently. It's a shame for him, really. Even at Asda the other day, when he eventually got served after queuing a while, the checkout girl said, 'Sorry about your weight.'

9th November 2011

Happy birthday, Poppy, my small dangly-eared friend. I hope you roll in something really nasty on your special day.

14th November 2011

I love our Monday-morning fun race. Can Dad lock the servatree door before the windowcleany man gets here? If not, we play with his bucket of water. If Dad does lock the door, I get to bark at the windowcleany man and jump up at the windows. It's funny but, whichever game we play, the windowcleany man always goes a funny pale colour... he-he.

15th November 2011

It says everyone has a skill. I think mine is counter surfing with stealth. I know some dogs prefer the full-on worktop offensive, and full respect to them, but I like the ninja mode myself. Wander round picking out the edible goodies by nose; zero in by sight; quietly up on the back legs; front paws onto the counter, and tongue and teeth do the rest. This approach has minimal telling-off risk and even some hidden admiration from the hoomans if they catch me in the act...

16th November 2011

Canine friends, beware 'the glass'. I think it's a new weapon that the hoomans have invented to see us when we're norty. I was climbing on the kitchen table this morning to clean up after the mini-hoomans when Dad said, 'Get down!' Nobody was about, so I thought he was singing again. Then he said, 'Monty, get down, I can see you.' So I got down and checked out where he was, and he was in the uvver room. I heard him say to Mum, 'I knew he was on that table, I could see him in the glass.' Sneaky, sneaky hoomans.

18th November 2011

Just realised this is the first time I've been left on my own at home for two hours. Mmm, now how shall I keep myself entertained? Tell me again, how do you open that fridge?

19th November 2011

Now I see some stuff livings with these hoomans of mine, but what's even stranger is living with the Cockeyed Spangles. I'm a simple sort of chap; when I need to do my business it's out in the garden, bombs away and then back in the house. With Molly and Bailey, though, it's like an art form. They do, synchronised number twos. I kid you not, they go round in little circles and then do their business at exactly the same time. It's freaky. I tell you what, if that becomes an Olympic event those two are gold-medal hopes for GB.

> For all of Monty's bad behaviour in the house and generally with me, he was becoming a very calm and well-socialised dog. This was highlighted when we met a man with a rescue Old English Sheepdog that had had a really bad start in life.

20 November 2011

Made a new friend today. I was out for a walk with Dad when we met Charlie and his dad. Charlie is an old Inglish Sheepish Dog who had been treated really bad by his last mum and dad and was locked in a shed for three years and beaten. He has something called 'fear aggression' and wanted to kill me. I knew he never meant it though, so I let him have a good bark and growl and just chilled. We spent about two hours together and we were good mates in the end. Poor old Charlie, but he has a nice kind dad now.

22nd November 2011

On me walk last night, a dog had a go at me. No reason, just being nasty. Poobag said it was a cross Staffie. Well, he's lucky he didn't see a very cross Monty.

I don't mind Staffies, I'm not one of those breedists. I just don't like cross dogs, but I don't like cross people either...

23rd November 2011

Just had a play with a Booby Day in Flanders. He was a big dog and his dad said he was a bit scared of me. I don't know why he was scared because I wasn't pulling my scary face.

24th November 2011

Watch out for them vetandhairypeople. When I went I only had a cough, but he shoved a thermometer up me backside. He said it was fine. Well, it might be for you but I didn't find it fine at all, mate.

25th November 2011

Had a fight with a clothes airy thingybob last night. I was asleep minding my own business and the crazy thing leapt on me. I ran into Mum and Dad. I wasn't scared, just checking it wasn't going to attack them.

26th November 2011

I had a dream last night. Dad said I woke him up growling and thrashing me legs around. Well, it's not every day you have to fight off a crocodicadial while you're swimming in the lake. I saw what they do to them williebeests on the wildwife programmes.

Anyone who has lived with Newfies, or any double-coated breed, will know the feeling of being continually cold. It seems that even the middle of winter with howling gales doesn't mean the back door can be shut.

27th November 2011

Nice breeze today. Why do hoomans keep shutting the windows? I have to keep getting up and opening the back door. I'm trying to get some sleep here.

Had me walk this morning and then an hour sitting outside Sainysburys doing me social I station. If one more person calls me a pony...

> Cocking his leg became a bit of a challenge for Monty. It's not surprising really, considering how he was growing – he was certainly at a gangly stage.

28th November 2011

I had a wee today on three legs. Not sure why, and it felt a bit wobbly, but it just happened. Maybe I'll try it again sometime.

1st December 2011

My dad said his school report read, 'A boy with much potential but who makes so little effort he is destined for a menial job waiting on others.' Dad, when is my food ready? I want to get out for a walk. Oh and by the way there's some poo in the garden you haven't picked up yet. Teachers – they know, don't they?

Whoops, somebody managed to get the mince pies off the cooker and eat one. It wasn't me, even though Dad said I'm the only one that can reach. Innocent until proved guilty, hooman. Don't you know the law?

4th December 2011

Spent some time outside Sainysbury's in Doncaster today. It's a little town in Yorkiepudshire and everyone goes, 'Thee's a big lad, tha'll need a saddle soon.' I'm used to funny voices 'cos I come from Wigwam, so it's OK.

I knocked over a big poster thingy but that wasn't my fault because I was getting fusses. I did eat an old lady's receipt but Dad says maybe he'll get Nectar points when he gets my poo up.

5th December 2011

This three-legged weeing isn't quite as easy as it first appears. I need to stand further away from the hedge because when I try to lift my leg I fall over. It's all a bit embarrassing really.

> Our first Christmas with a giant dog that could reach everything proved a challenge when putting up the decorations. We learnt later this is a problem faced by many Griswoldians the world over.

14th December 2011

Our house was suddenly turned into a scene from a Cwissymouse card, with stuff everywhere. Dad said the flashing things on the indoor tree were plugged into the wall and if I tried any of the three-legged weeing stuff I'd get a poodle coat. He doesn't usually buy me presents. Have to give that a go later.

Getting into the cwissymouse spirit

17th December 2011

Mum went out last night, so Dad had a night in with a curry and few drinks. Mum said, 'Good luck, Monty.' I didn't know what she meant. There was loads of room on the bed but he started doing his duck impressions under the covers again... I slept in the kitchen.

18th December 2011

Got hooman relatives coming to visit today. They've never seen me before so it's best behaviour from me. Ha-ha, who am I kidding?

Welcome from a dull and dreary Wigwam. By the way, the weather is even worse.

Hello Nanny Cuckoo

21st December 2011

Wet and windy, my favourite walking weather. Lots of pieces of paper and flying schoolchildren to chase after.

I think I might get lots of pressies. My hoomans love me lots and I've been a good boy this year – well, almost all year. Dad is cooking the Cwissymouse dinner with Poobag so there will be lots left once they scrape the burnt stuff off, he-he.

22nd December 2011

I am not happy at all about the three-legged weeing stuff. I tried to practise on a big bush in a garden this morning but ended up sitting on top of it and the people in the house were looking funny at me. Dad said I squashed it all down. It was an accident... Sorry.

I'm going for a walk very soon. I like looking at the pwetty lights round the streets. There are lots of different colours and they flash on and off. Mum once said Dad looks OK in the right light. I keep looking ... not seen it yet.

> We started to see how this attention Monty was getting when he was out in public could be used for good causes.

23rd December 2011

Just got back from me usual shopping trip. I was helping the Rotary Club tonight. You make a donation and you cuddle Monty. Phew, I am all cuddled out.

28th December 2011

Three-legged weeing update. Got it sorted now: lift one leg and wee. Seems simple enough. Dad is picky. He says it should be the back leg and not the front one. You can't please some people, can you?

29th December 2011

I'm just about to go for a walk. Chasing leaves is just soooo hard to stop doing. I try really hard, but then one flies past and ... and ... and I have to chaaaaase it. My name is Monty and I can't stop chasing leaves. I feel better now.

Dad is trying to train me, ha-ha. Now, that funny noise he makes is interesting 'cos then he gives me a treat when I look at him and the treats are nice. But those leaves ... gotta chase 'em

Not been called lush before, unless that's short for little git. I've been called that before a few times.

30th December 2011

Bailey has to go to the vets next week for a small operation. My eyes have started to water already... I won't make any jokes about it, I'll just be here for him. What? I mean it.

2012

1st January 2012

My New Year's resolution is to be kinder to those less fortunate than myself. That'll be the Cockeyed Spangles and me dad.

2nd January 2012

Wondering if I may blow away today. Looking at the wind direction, I could end up in Eddies Burrow (that's in Scotchland). Can you look out for me? I look like a big furry magpie with a little fat bloke dangling on the other end of the lead.

3rd January 2012

Been for me walk, didn't blow away. Good job Dad enjoyed his Cwissymouse sooo much, cos that extra weight kept us on the ground. I did the whole walk without me horse collar thingy. Dad said I was a good boy and kept giving me treats, but they were rubbish. If anyone know some nice treats to help with his training, can you let me know. Ta xx

OK, the dadster made me a new treat to help with me training him. Sardine cake, not bad considering he made it himself. I have got fish breath now, though. That's it, lots of sloppy kisses for me hoomans tonight me thinks.

CHAPTER 5
Gridlock In York

Monty's journey through doggy adolescence had turned a cute puppy into a hormone-driven beast. On many occasions it made us question our decision to own a giant breed. We were certainly finding out things they don't always tell you in the books.

4th January 2012

This three-legged weeing just gets more and more complicated and there is so much to learn. OK, lift the BACK leg and wee... Check. Don't actually jump on or in the bush else it gets squashed... Check. That's it I've learned. No, there's more? Lift back leg and do lots of small wees and not one big long wee for two minutes that runs all down someone's drive and gets Dad mad.

But wait there's more. Don't wee up the car wheel when there is someone sitting in it, that gets him mad too... I never saw the man in the car complaining. I wish someone would write a book so I could learn it all. I may just go back to puppy squatting.

I've been norty today. I have been growly, barky, bolshy and bitey. Mum and Dad said they were godamsickoffme and were going to give me away to a bad home. Don't think they mean it. Well, at least I don't think so. Nah, surely they can't ... can they?

Don't like these addielessons, they make me go crazy.

5th January 2012

If anyone gets kisses from me licckle bruvver Bailey, you will be pleased to know that he hasn't just licked his boy bits and never will again. Sorry, bruv, couldn't resist that one.

7th January 2012

Met a nice Greathound today. He had been tied to a post when he couldn't race anymore, which is really not nice. The hoomans who did that should have their men bits cut off and tied to one of those little mechanical hares ... or am I being harsh?

The hooman with the Greathound said we could have a run together off lead. Ha-ha I may look stupid, I may even be with stupid ... but that is never going to happen.

8th January 2012

Hoping I grow a bit taller 'cos then I can lick the kitchen table without jumping, but still have to stretch up a bit to reach the kitchen counter. Dad says I won't get taller, just get a big fat arse. Should I tell him or do you want to?

Just been for a walk in the rain and met two girls all dressed in pink. They made some funny noises. The first one was 'Awwwww'. Now this means they want cuddles. Then 'Arghhhhh'. This means 'he's very heavy and very wet'. Finally 'Urghhhh' which means 'have you seen the state of me trackie?'. Girls are funny things, really. Hope you're making notes fellow doglets, these hoomans are hard work and there is much to learn.

> Despite his adolescent behaviour at home, Monty was great with everyone he met and really patient when meeting smaller dogs that reacted unpredictably.

11th January 2012

Got attacked yesterday on me walk. I was bouncing around and wanting to play with Sam when he got grumpy, and next thing I knew he was attached to me. Whoah, calm down little fella. I was only playing. Luckily, he hasn't got too many teeth and I've got me big woolly coat on, so I didn't feel a thing. Next time I may just sit on him.

Just had a scare on me walk. A hooman drove up to us, stopped got out and came over. I thought it was the man from the house where I just weed up his bush come to tell me off. He wasn't telling me off though, just wanted to say hello and give me some treats and then drove off again. I know I've said this before, but hoomans are strange creatures.

12th January 2012

It's sunny, must be time for a walk. I have places to go and people to meet, hooman servant; please fetch me my lead and away we go, there's a good fellow. You see, you have to know how to talk to these bipeds.

How embarrassing was that? On me walk three young ladies were walking a fine-looking Beagly so I thought I'd mark my territory to show who's the big boy round here... Unfortunately, I forgot to lift that back leg and peed all over me front legs. I moved off really quick. I'm sure nobody saw... What? It could happen to anyone.

13th January 2012

I love the squeaky mini-hoomans. You bite various places and they squeak dead good. They squeak when you sit on them too. Funny, funny things.

As my doggie friends know, this is my first time owning hoomans and I just wanted some advice. Should they be better trained by now? The dad one still pulls on the lead and is a bit slow with the treats sometimes. He can also get stroppy from time to time. Is that just a phase he's going through? My main problem is when we meet other hoomans it takes me ages to get him away, he just wants to do hooman talking. Any advice would be great. Ta.

15th January 2012

Not my most successful walk this morning. Note to self when looking at birdies fly ,watch out for parked cars... Ouch, another dent. The other thing is that when having the three-legged wee, make sure nobody's foot is there. Sorry, Poobag.

16th January – my first birthday

Today is me buffday, and I am a whole one year old. I got extra treats but had to share with the miniature dangly-eared ones. Apart from that, it was good day t. I wonder if they'll be even smaller when I'm two?

One today. Who's a big boy then?

My thought for the day: Some people go through life treating others like crab. They sea them as nothing, just prawns in their little game. Who are they squidding, though? We all know they are just shellfish.

17th January 2012

I am a very tolerant Newfie. I try not to stare at the Spangles' ears because I realise it's just the way that nature made them.

20th January 2012

Raining all day today in Happy Town. Poor hoomans, all those extra clothes to put on. Me? I'll be modelling a rather fetching all-in-one, black-and-white waterproof with fitted hat, gloves and boots.

We thought when Monty first came it would be nice if he could come in and out of our bedroom. That thought didn't last too long.

22nd January 2012

I have worked out that if I roll up in a little ball I can fit on the pillows between Mum and Dad at night. It's very comfy. I can't stay long though, 'cos of the snoring. It keeps me awake. Flippin' hoomans. I never knew they'd be this noisy.

26th January 2012

My personal favourite is weeing on my legs in the garden and then jumping on the bed. I find this usually gets them up.

30th January 2012

I got called an Old English sheepdog yesterday. Unless – mmm, maybe they meant Dad. Now I come to think of it, there are some similarities.

Stood outside the bunny show yesterday doing me socially-ice-station stuff. Meeting people with licckle bunny wabbits and pinny gigs. Everyone said how good I was. But they didn't know what I was thinking...

3rd February 2012

The man building the wall on me walk yesterday was nice. He stopped working and said, 'He's a great dog,' then he gave me a fuss and wanted to play, so we did. Then he went over the wall he was building and disappeared into the garden. Sorry, did I knock you over a bit? Oops, clumsy me.

6th February 2012

Bailey thought it was safe playing with squeaky duck in his crate. Mwa-ha-ha-ha, wrong, chocolate-teapot boy. If you pull hard enough you can get anything to fit through those bars. Now it's MINE.

11th February 2012

Love is never getting told off when I jump on Mum and Dad's bed at night six or seven times. Never moaning when I tread on them, squeeze between them and leave hair all over their pillow. They don't even moan when I give them sloppy kisses just after I've had a drink of water. They must really love me.

13th February 2012

I think it's fair enough if Dad is eating malty-easers that I jump on him, pin him down and try to help him share them. Just 'cos they're in his mouth doesn't mean to say they are his. Funnily he doesn't agree...

15th February 2012

Guess how many Valleytimes cards I got yesterday??? Well it ended with zero ... and guess what? It started with zero too. You ever seen a big puppy dog sobbing?

It seemed that just going out with Monty was an adventure. The reaction he got from people and dogs was fascinating and often unpredictable. The Farcebook page continued to grow as more and more people joined and read his daily stories.

11th March 2012

Busy day for me today. Been for a walk at Wigwam Flashes, then another walk up at Haigh Hall with lots of hoomans and mini-hoomans. Then I went on a trip to a Sainysburys and sat outside while Mum and Poobag went shopping. There was a mini-hooman who couldn't walk and had a lead on like me. She was tiny weenie licckle, and kept coming up looking at me. She got dead close and was pointing at me and wanting kisses. I couldn't though 'cos me kisses would knock her over, so I played it cool and pretended she wasn't there. It was OK – she went ... after about twenty minutes. Phew, time for a kip methinkszzzzzzzzzzzzzz

30th March 2012

They must have heard there was going to be a shortage of Cockeyed Spangles. Mum and Dad panic bought. They are everywhere in this house.

6th April 2012

Me icckle bruvver Bailey is going on summat called a home check tomorrow. It's to see that a little puppy Spangle is going to a good home and Dad wants to show them the worstest Cockeyed Spangle ever. If they can cope with an hour of Bailey, they can survive anything.

13th April 2012

Got attacked today by a Lassie asbo. I kept my cool and just wagged me tail but that wound him up even more. I was like Cassie-arse Clay on the ropes – 'bring it on sucker, that all you got?' His mum and dad said it hates me, and even barks every time it sees me through the window. That's not nice is it? So much anger.

14th April 2012

I was joined on me afternoon walk by Minnie Spangle puppy, being carried. Lazy little devil. We are looking after her till her new mum and dad come back from hollydaze. We need to sociallyize her so she doesn't turn out like me. That's what Dad said. Is he being nice or nasty? I can never tell.

26th April 2012

Just tried to play with a one eyed Shitty-zoo but he ran away. Sadly he was on his lead and ran straight into his mum 'cos he couldn't see her legs. Ouch. Poor little chap. Sorry, licckle guy.

9th May 2012

Went off into the woods today to chase a sqwibbel. Nearly got it too, using my stealth mode. Then he just ran up a tree – how's that fair? Thought I'd keep running round the woods though, 'cos it was fun, but all of a sudden I found I couldn't walk. I was OK once Dad got all the branches off me. He said I looked like I was camel-tarred or summat.

16th May 2012

My mum and dad are buying me something called a cartoon-ourness. It goes on me back and then I pull a thing with wheels on, or summat. Dad thinks it will be good for me. Well, just as long as that lardy boy don't try to get on, I should be OK.

13th June 2012

Molly Spangle did a runner on her walk today ... again! She just disappears in the woods, legs it and then comes back home an hour later. Does she get told off?? Never. Those Cockeyed dangly ones are really norty and they get away with it. Me? I do one thing wrong and I'm bad, bad Monty. It's not fair.

Saw me licckle enemy the Sharp-hay on me walk today. He hates me for some reason but I don't like him either. I gave him the big Monty growl 'RAAAAAARRRRRRRRRRRRRRR'. Ha-ha, he pooed himself. Take that you, little wrinkly Chinese bully.

> Our trip to York was one of the most bizarre days out we've had with Monty. In the city centre a coach full of Chinese tourists all wanted their picture taken with him. One by one. One got down next to him while the other forty stood in the main road to take the photo. The city centre was gridlocked and some of the tourists got more than they'd bargained for.

20th June 2012

Going on a day trip to a place called Yorkie today. Mum wants to go shopping and Dad says he wants to socialite me with sum soffiticated people. Good luck with that one, old man. He says there is a big church made out of choclite, called Yorkie Mister. Is he telling the truth? If he is it sounds delicious.

I am officially a Yorkie tourist attraction. I am so tired now. Been having me piccie taken all day with lots of people who spoke lots of different langyjizz. It was bad when they all blocked the road to take pictures of me, and one girl wanted one pretending to kiss me. Sorry, you don't just pretend to kiss Monty... I had to give her a Newfydoof special and she couldn't get up off the pavement. Oh, what fun I've had.

A well-deserved Ice Cream   I told you I was famous

26 June 2012

Newfydoof vs fly ... round 1 to the fly but I'll be back, me licckle winged snack.

1st July 2012

Mum and Dad went shopping yesterday without me. They saw two of Bernie's mounting dogs. They said they were lovely and spent ages fussing them. I wonder how many mounting dogs this Bernie has got???

5th July 2012

When Dad got down on the floor, I thought he was playing our game of 'Hooman lies on the floor and I jump all over them'. I didn't know he had hurt his leg and couldn't stand up. Whoops. He's back from hooman hospital now and he has got two extra legs too. He still loves me though.

CHAPTER 6
Two Stone Lighter

Monty was certainly becoming hard work at times because of his male urges. It made things difficult around other male dogs, so we decided to try an implant. The idea was that if the implant helped the situation but didn't affect his personality, we could safely go ahead with neutering. We felt this was the best course of action. Obviously, Monty had plenty to say about it.

23rd July 2012

I have to go to the vetandhairyman this afternoon. They are putting a plant in me to stop me thinking of girls. Hope it's not a stinging nettle or nuffin like that. Dad says it won't hurt. I'll just feel a little prick... Well, he'd know, wouldn't he?

24th July 2012

Had me plant in yesterday but I still like the girls. Dad says it will take time for me testy-on-the-phone to go away and then I will be a happy boy. It was at the new vetandhairyman place. I was a good boy yesterday but when the lady behind the desk said, 'Hello Gorgeous,' I had to jump up for a kiss, didn't I? There was no room to squeeze through so I had to make some... Whoops. I didn't sit in the water bowl yesterday though, so I'm getting better.

17th August 2012

Back to the vetandhairyman today. He was a bit rude and was feeling me undercarriage. He said they've shrunk a bit. Well, you never let me check you, Mr Vetty; maybe yours ain't so big. I gotta have another tin-plant in a few weeks. The nursey lady said hello gorgeous in the waity room so I jumped up for a kiss ... again. I didn't mean to knock those flowery things and the water on the floor. Dad said I'm gonna get banned – that suits me. No more touchy-feely vet boy.

9th September 2012

Poppy keeps shoving her bum into my face. Mmm, not sure the implant thingy bob works 'cos even though she's a ginger Cockeyed Spangle it still smells very interesting... Dirty girl!

10th September 2012

Just enjoying that doggy programme on TV and was getting into it when a huge dog appeared behind me. He was horrible with a big slobbery face, and I had to growl to scare him off. He had a scary name too. Poobag said he was called myflection.

11th September 2012

Off to the vetandhairyman today as I am poorly. Got a bad tummy and lots of squirty number twos. Hope he don't say to starve me, that would be a disaster.

That's it, been to vetandhairyman. I have to be starved for twenty-four hours... I'm wasting away, I am. At this rate I'll be Spangle-sized soon.

12th September 2012

Three hours twenty minutes till food time ... not that I'm counting.

14th September 2012

Molly, me licckle Spangle sister, went to the vet's tonight for a check-up. Mum and Dad came back saying she'd been norty and had 'gone for a Snawtzer'. I went for one earlier and it was solid and they said I was a good boy, so what's going on there? Tch ... hoomans, they drive me crazy.

18th September 2012

I woke up this morning and decided I would like to chase every car, van and bus that went past on our walk. I saw that ad on the teglyvision fingy and it said 'try something new today'.

19th September 2012

Can't stop eating the fings on the fridge door at the moment. There is something I can't resist about them ... it's almost magnetic.

2nd October 2012

Two days till I move into the new house with Mum and Dad. I am a bit excited ... OK, very excited. The dangly-eared ones are coming two days later so it gives me time to get me paws under the table...

3rd October 2012

The skirty boards in the new house were all new and had no chew marks in them at all. Don't worry, they have now. Now it feels like home.

18th October 2012

Cos we've moved, I do a new walk in the morning. It's past about six billion school-hoomans. I can share slobber, hair and kisses, whether they want them or not.

There is a Shitty-zoo that hates me and barks and barks every time he sees me. I was out on a walk with me dad and we met him and he was better than usual. His dad picked him up and said he'd heard that if he held him next to me, it would help him be calmer. He couldn't remember which end so he gave me the bum end to have a sniff. Phew, thank dog for that – I didn't fancy that other end ... there's teeth in there, mate.

With Monty coming up to two, we made the decision to get him some similar sized company and contacted a lovely breeder in Newcastle. Cookie would be arriving soon to add some more 'interest to his life'– but first to sort out his little problem.

A New baby sister

How cute

19th November 2012

Morning. Yesterday was interesting. Wonder what surprises the hoomans have for me today now they've got me a sista sorted. I would have been happy with a biscuit, honest.

Dad came back from walking the Spangles this morning saying Poppy had eaten some poo, rolled in some and was fighting with Bailey. Molly wouldn't listen to anything he said... Oh, and I'm the problem one, am I?

20th November 2012

Me tinplant thingy that stop me thinkling of the girls has ran out. Dad said it should have lasted till Janny-welly but it's run out already. Good news is Dad says I'm not having another one. He said I won't need to worry about it anymore, he's fixing it for good... That's good news? Right?

What do you mean dad, fixing it for good?

21st November 2012

Dad booked me in yesterday for hoppyration. The lady behind the desk said, 'Ooh, Monty, you'll come out two-stone lighter,' then she laughed... I don't get it. What does she mean, peoples?

24th November 2012

Bayleaf, the evil brown Cockeyed Spangle, told me I should have a day chilling, just licking my balls. He said it's polite to take the time to say goodbye to old friends. I hate him. No, really I do.

25th November 2012

Been to the shops today. I met lots of nice hoomans. One lady was very sad because her dog had died not long ago. I gave her loads of slobbery kisses and she said, 'Thank you so much, I've missed that.' There are some nice hoomans about.

27th November 2012

Well, today's the day. Wish me luck. I'll try to be brave. Wonder if I get to pick what's on TV later. Ooh, Turner and Hooch, Turner and Hooch ... it's me favvyreet.

I'm back. I'm very sleepy and feeling sorry for myself. I wuz very brave, though. They gave me a needle in me leg and it made me sleepy, but I still managed to get on the big table before I fell asleep. I've got chicken for tea so I'm happppyyyyzzzzzzzzzz

28th November 2012

Chicken for breakfast as well. Oh, I am so lucky. Lots of tablets, too. Dad thinks he hides them, ha-ha. I just eat them. I like him to win one challenge a day.

2nd December 2012

Getting rid of some of my magazines 'cos I don't think I'll be needing them anymore. There's Puppies Galore ... Bitches on Heat ... Big Newfie Girls ... Bad, Bad Girl (Christmas edition) and me book the Canine Sutra Lurrry Positions for Liberal-Minded Doglets. This is the new edition which includes a step-by-step guide to 'doing it hooman style'.. just PM me for further details.

4th December 2012

Went back to the doggy docs yesterday to get checked out. The vetandhairyman asked if I'd lay down so he could have a look. Please, I wasn't falling for that one again. In the end he slid underneath me like one of them car-maniac people. I was waiting for him to mess with me big end... He'd have been wearing a big black-and-white Newfydoof hat for a few weeks if he had.

I am on Twitter now. Dad says I should go on because I am already a big twit. I really don't understand what he's talking about most of the time.

5th December 2012

The lovely Spangles spent their whole walk this morning eating bird seed that somebody had put on the floor at regular intervals. They have been sick all afternoon and have poo that looks like those budgie treats you hang up... I love Spangles, they make me look like a genie-arse.

7th December 2012

Just seen the three Lassie-asbos that always bark at me. I lay down and they kept coming nice and quiet. They couldn't see me because of the sun. I came at them like a Messy-shit pilot and jumped up to say hello... Poor things screamed like Dad when he's see's Mum's shopping bill. Their hooman is still picking up the poo... Sorry, not sorry.

8th December 2012

Been for a walk today along the carnal. Then we went into Wigwam town centre to practise me sociaicestation. Dad said if I can behave around wild Wigwammers I'm a good boy. It's those pigeons I can't handle, all that cooing and then they fly off. If only I had wings, they'd be cooing on the other side of their beaks.

On me way home from town, the man in the burger van said, 'What a handsome lad.' He wanted his wife to take photo of him giving me a sausage ... whoa, Tiger. I may have had the op but I still like the girls. Norty boy!

12th December 2012

Dad has had mansickness, which he says is worse than the manflu. It sounds bad. I hope I don't get it. He better get up and take me for a walk or else he'll have monty-sits-on-yer-till-yer-get-up-ya-lazy-git-itis.

CHAPTER 7
The Joy Of A New Sister

Cookie arrived and so did Christmas, and she became part of the festive tradition of dressing up the dogs in holiday costumes. Monty always enjoyed this sooo much.

We all have to dress up Cookie

One day you may look as cool as me

17th December 2012

Really not sure about me new sister. She's got lots of toys but doesn't like sharing. She collected them all up and took them to her den. I can only just get me head in there, so pinching them is difficult.

I told her to cry when she wakes up then wait till Dad comes and wee just before he can open the door. It'll be really funny and the hoomans love it. Did she listen? Dad comes down, she wags her tail, 'Hello, Dad,' and then goes outside and does a wee. All I can hear is, 'Good girl, Cookie...' Creep.

27th December 2012

Well, that's the Christmas stuff over with. Maybe now the two-legged ones will stop dressing us up. I have a reputation, you know. Do you know how hard it is to look cool with felt antlers stuck on yer head?

30th December

Cookie had her first trip to the vetandhairyman yesterday. Silly girl got her face stuck trying to chew the bars on the gate. She hurt her licckle nose and was feeling all sorry for herself. Vetandhairyman gave her a magic needle and she was back to super norty again. I liked her more yesterday...

2013

13th January 2013

This having a sister lark ain't all what it's cracked up to be. She'll be a playmate for you, they said. She'll be company, they said. Well, she's got teeth like razors and she never stops, she just keeps going like the flippin' Durex-hell bunny.

She never stops

Cookie Monster has her jab tomorrow. She's had her first one, so she knows it's only a little needle. Don't tell her, but I think she's getting the microwave insert done too. You wait till you see how big that bad boy is!

15th January 2013

What is this hooman of mine doing now? I used to eat me brekky in three seconds flat, so he went and bought me a new bowl called a 'slow feeder'. It's like a mazey fing. I have to chase me biccy fings all round the place and it take me ages. They spoil all my fun.

> We had been told by lots of Newfoundland owners that two was the magic number and we hoped Monty would begin to settle and be a little less destructive. Well, it's nice to have hope, isn't it?

16th January 2013 – Monty's second Birthday

Dad just went to Tesco to get something for his sore throat. He should have gone to the stables 'cos he was a little hoarse... I do make meself chuckle sometimes.

Two today, whoopy-doo! A new sister plus the Spangles, could life get any worse? Even the buffday treats didn't bring much pleasure. OK, they were very nice but don't tell the hoomans 'cos I'm still sulking.

Me birthday cake had a candle on top on fire. Did they expect me to blow it out? I did make a wish though. Dog dammit, he's still here.

Thanks everyone for my birthday wishes, it was very kind. I had a great day but didn't eat all the cake. I did share some with the Spangles 'cos they need feeding up and then maybe they'll grow a bit. Cookie had some too but she don't need to grow a bit, she's doing that all by herself. Had a lovely day but now I'm tiredzzzzzzzzzzzzzz

That cake looks too good to share

I'm two today. I think you three are getting smaller

A new sister and spangles. Happy birthday Monty.

18th January 2013

I think everyone should leave Tesco alone now. They have apologised and vowed to get to the bottom of the horse-meat burger scandal... In fact yesterday they launched an immediate stewards' enquiry.

Police in Wigwam have warned the public about severe disruption in the borough due to the arctic weather conditions. Two millimetres of snow fell overnight and, whilst they admitted there is likely to be disruption to emergency services, schools and roads, they were quick to reassure everyone PIE SHOPS WILL REMAIN OPEN. They also dismissed rumours that somebody was seen wearing long trousers.

19th January 2013

I like this white stuff. I do a number two and then go round it slowly, piling the snow on top with me nose till it's hidden. Bingo, it's a poopy trap. Well, everyone's gotta have a hobby.

Walk off the lead today. I had a great run through the woods in the snow. They used to be woods, now they're called clearings... Whoops

21st January 2013

Proper snow for us today. The true Wigwam folk are still going dressed as usual...That's vest and pants, although because of the cold they are wearing socks with their sandals... And that's the women.

Watch you don't slip Dad

*You're not meant
to eat it Cookie.*

24th January 2013

Finally found something good about having a sister that bites me all of the time. She gets a treat every time she goes out for a wee, and I get one too. She does about fifteen piddles an hour. Happy days.

27th January 2013

Dad can't understand why I have to climb onto the top of piles of snow in the garden to have a wee. Hoomans, you don't have to understand everything. Some things are just fun.

28th January 2013

OK, so if I had to choose between a new sister, another Bailey or pulling my own teeth out? Anybody got some pliers?

31st January 2013

I overheard Mum and Poobag talking this morning. I'd been expecting it, but the words still hit me hard. 'I think it's best if we rehome him. Now we have the puppy we just don't have the time. He eats so much ... and then there's the mess round the house. Yes, but who would want him? He's so bad with people, he's just a big useless lump.' Well that is harsh, but I have to agree it would be better if Dad had another home. I'm gonna miss him, though.

1st February 2013

Guess who wanted a poo at half past five this morning? The biting I can take, but I need me beauty sleep, Junior.

5th February 2013

Wow, that really tired me out today. Maisey, the Boxy dog, is dead fast and she can wrestle dead good for a girl. Think I may have a quiet night tonight with a bit of telly and Mum-and-Dad cuddles.

14th February 2013

Mum and Dad have gone away for a while so I'm left with Poobag, the mini-hoomans the Spangles and the Cookie Monster. At least there's somebody responsible here.

25th February 2013

Been up the learning zoo to meet the mini-hoomans. Wow, they love them slobbery kisses, I thought I may not have enough to go round. Note to self – must drink more water before I go next time.

28th February 2013

You know when you've missed someone? When you haven't seen your beloved pet for a while? When you just want to kiss that hairy face and see that slobber everywhere? That's how I feel. I'll be seeing dad tomorrow. Can't wait.

1st March 2013

Mum and Dad are back. Guess what? No pressies yet. I didn't throw myself at them but gave em the Newfydoof bum waggle. Only half kisses, though – they did leave me after all. Maybe if there are pressies tomorrow there will be full kisses. Maybe.

I missed you guys really.

One thing we realised quite quickly is that living with a giant dog affected things like the size of car you have. When you have two giant dogs, obviously things change again. What were we thinking?

4th March 2013

Mum and Dad went to look at a new car today. They took me to see if I could fit in the back. Mum said, 'Look, if we pull the headrest up, we won't even need a guard. They'll never get through there.' If ever I've heard a challenge...

Well, guess what? They'll need a guard. Can't make it too easy for these hoomans.

I did feel a bit sorry for the salesman 'cos he was sitting on the back seat as I tested the easy Newfydoof hurdle. I don't think he liked me sitting on his lap. The squealy grunty noises he made kinda gave it away.

> Walking had become a military exercise with five dogs with different needs to accommodate. Then there was the socialisation to keep on top of. Having a baby sister took it out of Monty, who developed a limp. It wasn't the last time Cookie would run him ragged.

9th March 2013

I hurt me leg tonight playing with the heffalump. I was on the couch then suddenly I was eating carpet. I bet she tripped me, the sneaky little monster. It did hurt, but I didn't let on to Her Hairiness.

Who's the boss?

11th March 2013

Yesterday I managed to get hold of a plant Mum bought from the gardie centre. It was called a bunnysuckle. I chewed it up a bit and spat it out. Mum and Dad got all panicky 'cos they said it was poysnuss to dogs. I got special fusses and they kept watching me all night. They read one of the simpytums is losing your appytight. They kept trying me with treats every few hours to check I hadn't lost it. I must eat more plants.

12th March 2013

So, walking down the road I passed a lady. I knew she liked me, but the Newfydoof eyes didn't do it and she carried on walking. OK, Plan P: Big bark, woo-woo-WOO, then she looks round. I do the massive Newfie bum waggle and loads of big hairy tail. Mwa-ha-ha, she was putty in me paw. Back she comes, big fuss, job done. Watch and learn, Cookie, me licckle apprentice.

13th March 2013

Me and Cookie both going up the learning zoo this morning. Just wanted to give the short-legged one a lesson in pulling a crowd. I hope Cookie's not too upset when I get all the children fussing me and she just has the company of the short-sighted mum who thinks she's a Chow.

14th March 2013

Well, what can I say? Learning zoo was ... an education. (Ha-ha, see what I did there?) Why was I surrounded by children while Cookie was on her own? Lesson 1: When you have a six-inch shoelace of Newyfdoof goo hanging from your face that has been collecting stuff from the floor, just wipe it on Dad's leg. That's what he's there for. The big hoomans don't like it on the mini-ones' schoolie ooniforms. There endeth today's lesson, young Jedi.

Been out for a walk in the rain and the dark... wooooh! Cookie was a licckle bit scared, bless her. I barked at a few cars just to add to the atmosphere of scariness. Cookie, you ain't seen scary yet. Wait till Dad gets his shorts on, now that is scary.

15th March 2013

Cookie is going to vetandhairyman today to get weighed. It'll be the last time. Next time it's the zoo. Well, they must have to weigh the hippos.

Mum is giving Molly a haircut again. These Spangles don't half get some pamperising. I'm lucky if I get a haircut once a mumf. Bailey gets his eyelashes curled one a week. Poppy has her lug'oles combed all the time. Even the fat little brown one gets loads of baffs. That's because she sits in her own wee. Dirty little hippo.

16th March 2013

Rainy in Wigwam this morning – how shocked am I? Not that it bothers me, but it does make the hoomans grumpy. I know, it's hard to believe that Mr Sweetness and Light aka Dad gets grumpy, but he does when it's raining ... and when it's windy ... and when it's cold... Oh and when it's warm, and when it's dry.

Me and the Cookster been for a nice sqwelshy wet walk and she actually behaved herself. People in cars keep waving and smiling at us. Dad waves back, he thinks he's really popular. Should I break it to him?

17th March 2013

What's all this teething stuff about? Playing with Cookie last night, I looked like I'd been in a shark attack. Dad said I was like a newspaper. Black and white and read all over. He said it was a joke... He says some strange things. Mum yawns a lot.

Me and the hairy hippo have been to the garding centre. That lady bent down for a kiss but I fort she was giving me a treat. OK, it was a plant thing she was holding but I didn't know. It didn't taste nice so I didn't chew, just held it, honest. Dad told me to leave, so I did – eventually. It did make a bit of a mess on the floor. Sorry... Again.

When we are out the hoomans say the same about me all the time. Dad sometimes says it about the hoomans and he larfs to himself. Look at him – I wouldn't want to feed him for a week. You could put a saddle on that. Wouldn't want that sitting on your lap. Bet he needs a lot of grooming. You must have a big house to fit him in. I don't think the hoomans would think Dad was funny if they heard him. I think he may get some of them knuckle sandwich things.

18th March 2013

Poobag walked me tonight cos Dad was doing the training with Cookiepotomus. Thought I'd make it interesting 'cos I didn't want her to get bored, so I chased a lorry and made a Snawtzer try and get run over, 'cos eating a car bumper was less scary than meeting me. Then I pooed in the middle of the road with a car coming. I think Poobag found it interesting enough.

21st March 2013

Been to see the vetandhairyman today. Dad said if he didn't have me he could buy a new Beemer. He said instead he has a Citroen Berlingo and is buying the vetandhairyman a new Beemer. He's lost me again. He talks the gobble-dee-gook.

28th March 2013

Just having a quiet wee in the garden and one of them Blackybirds landed on the fence next to me. Whoa, made both of us jump. Me out of me skin and birdy out of his feathers... Nearly turned me number one into a number two.

29th March 2013

I know it's Easter and strange things happened back in the old days, but me limp has disappeared. Maybe it's a miracle and the godperson did it for me. Or is it what Dad says, just a fluke, and it will come back. Hmm, mysterious.

OK, it's good Friday and I've tried, but tomorrow is definitely bad Saturday... Then It's norty Sunday and let's-go-crazy Monday. Welcome back fourth leg, time to party... Mwha-ha-ha.

My name is Monty Dogge and I haven't chased a car for four days. Erm, till tonight. I was weak, I know that now. So glad I joined K9 Car Chasers Anony-mouse...

31st March 2013

Been out for a walk with Cookie Monster and on the way back she kept falling over. Mum and Dad was worried cos they thought she was really poorly. She is a brown girl though, and she was trying to scratch her ear with her back hoof. Yes, while she was walking. Cookie, you is giving Newfydoofs a bad name. Only the Spangles do stuff like that.

1st April 2013

I thought that sister of mine was a bit strange trying to scratch her head with her back leg when walking but this is better … she can grab her own ear and suck it. She then sits there with it in her mouth like a dummy. What is really funny is when she can't make her mind up which ear and shakes her head from side to side really fast and tries to catch one… She looks like a big furry smellycopter.

Like I said before she's a brown Newfydoof girl … I rest my case.

CHAPTER 8
A Hole In The Bag

Monty's limp seemed to come and go. Maybe having a boisterous sister wasn't helping, but our vet wanted Monty to see a specialist and they booked him in for an operation. We weren't comfortable with this and we decided to hold off and explore other options. Maybe like getting Cookie to calm down a bit. Thinking about it, maybe not that option.

2nd April 2013

Dad rang the specialips and cancelled me hoppyration, so I'm a happy boy. The only thing now is I'm taking more tablets than a hippocondriate. One of them is called Devils Claw. I wonder if I'll grow some horns?

4th April 2013

Me and Cookie are spending a little bit of time together again now. Last time I was chewing me deer-antler thingy and she wanted it, as usual. This time I did a big deep growl to tell her off. She left me — ha-ha, I won. Then all of a sudden I heard a big bark and she landed on me head, made me jump, dropped me bone and everything... She got it. I hate girls.

Dad took me and Cookie for a walk together this morning. We can't work out if he's brave or stoopid. I couldn't help it, that van was going too fast and I was telling it off. OK, so it was a norty thing to do and I sort of pulled ... a bit. Dad was angry and got us away from the road but I didn't fancy going and pulled the other way. Whoops! Me head collar thing fell off and everything went a bit apple-shaped.

Whew, everyone calmed down and Dad walked us home. I needed a poo. It's not my fault it was the middle of the road. Now Dad went different colours in his face and went to pick it up. He was saying some words I hadn't heard before. He was rushing so much his hand went through the bag. He's clever though and he didn't drop me poo – he had most of it on his hand. Now he had to get us both home with his hand in the air and holding us both in the other one.

I love our walks. He's a funny guy. He said he's donating me to the Foxy Fund Charity... They find doglets good homes. A good home, now that would be great.

Where did she come from?

5th April 2013

Been into town today to meet me hooman friends. I didn't jump up anybody, didn't bark once, didn't bounce on any other dogs. I didn't even chase a pigeon. I've been really, really good. That'll fool him ... till next time, mwa-ha-ha-ha.

6th April 2013

Just been for what Dad calls a training walk. Here's how it works. We walk on a busy road. I ignore the lorries and buses and I get a treat ... simples. After a bit though, if I just ignore them he says 'good boy' ... no treat. So here's what I have to do. I have to look interested in the lorry or bus and then stop meself like I'm really trying, just as it comes past. 'Good boy' ... treat. Really simples. I like the training walks, and I think he's learning.

7th April 2013

Had a play with Cookie Bear last night and me leg is stiff again this morning. Dad says I have to rest again. I hate resting, I like jumping and running, it's not fair.

Maybe I'll take up a new hobby. I was thinking maybe chess. It's a game for intelligent, sensitive individuals and those of us with planning skills. I guess I won't be playing Dad or Bailey then. Maybe I'll just write me memoirs.

9th April 2013

Watching the Horrorbit on telly last night with Mum and Dad. He's a small, strange creature with weird feet and a bit boring. Mum seems happy enough with him though. The film was quite enjoyable.

Mum and Dad sat next to each other on the sofa. WHAT? They know my place is in the middle getting durble fussed. Just sat on Mum's lap so she couldn't see. Then, like magic, they moved, ha-ha durble fusses. Then I got down and went to sleep on the floor. Mwa-ha-ha-ha.

10th April 2013

Had a little walk yesterday 'cos of me leg. Just a gentle stroll and a bit of sniffleing, a bit of watering of gateposts, and then I saw the windycleaner. Well, I have to say I don't like the windycleaner, he's always whistling, clanging his laddies and coming in the garden and not fussing me, so I stopped.

He was laffing and said to Dad, 'Ha-ha, he's not scared of the laddies, is he?' 'No,' said Dad. 'I think he wants to get you. Ha-ha.' Windyman walked in the road looking a bit sweaty.

Well, I couldn't resist... Rrarrr, and a couple of big whooo-whooo-whooos did the trick. Not scared of the big fluffy doggy, are you? Mwha-ha. Dad said bad boy ... again.

14th April 2013

Dad's still in bed 'cos he drank too much of the Scottyland falling-down water stuff last night, and we're all having to wait for our walks. I heard someone say he was a kisshead. I hope that means he's getting up soon.

> For some reason Monty seemed only ever to want to go to the toilet in the most inconvenient of places. His 'thing' became the middle of the road, and no matter how you tried to trick him it was like he was planning it.

I am perfecting delivering number twos in the middle of the road. It needs to be fairly quiet, but with the chance of a car coming. A bend is good, 'cos a car could come as a surprise and that worries Dad the most. He-he. I like to get right in the middle 'cos he shouts all the funny words then.

Been to the garding centre and Saneberrys today. I met lots of friends. I love the things Dad says. 'No, he's not a pony'(true). 'He eats less than the wife' (true). 'He's good most of the time' (hooge big fat lie).

16th April 2013

It's me noculation thingy-wotsit today. I have to have me elf check as well. I have to get on the scaleys and they say if I'm eating too much. Now doglets, here's a little trick for you. I just lean against the wall a bit and I always come out weighing the same as a Laberadoor. Eat on Monty, eat on...

Been to the vetandhairyman today. Did the waying stuff and I sat against the wall to be lighter and so get more food ... simples. Dad thought I'd lost too much weight 'cos I was only as heavy as a Chewywower and did it again. This time he was watching me close. BUSTED... Normal rations for me.

19th April 2013

So the hoomans are training the brown furball to be patient in the morning waiting for her food. Ha-ha. You'd have more success getting Bailey into Oxfyford Hoonyversity. Give up now hoomans, you will lose.

21st April 2013

I was allowed for a walk off me lead yesterday 'cos me leg is getting better. There was a Jack Rustly terror who looked like fun and I wanted to play. Poobag was worried, thought I'd be bouncy. Dad said don't worry he'll be fine. I was. I was fine chasing him. Poobag wasn't happy and stepped in front of me to stop me... Full speed Monty hits no speed Poobag... OUCH ... sorry.

22nd April 2013

Been up to the learning zoo this morning. There was another big doggy up there. Dad said it was a dog that was bored, though. I don't know why it was bored, maybe it needs a hobby.

One of me licckle hooman friends who cuddles me said, 'I don't love any other dogs in the world, only Monty.' Sorry other dogs in the world. Can I help it?

23rd April 2013

Mum and Dad just entered the Cookster into her first show. She's gonna be a show dog and get pampered and have loads of baths and stuff. Phew, I'm glad now that they chopped me nuts off. None of that stuff for this scruffy big Newfydoof bear.

OK, so I did try to chase that man on the bike – but did you hear what that Laberadoor that was with him said? 'I bet you wish you could run this fast, Lardy Arse.'

WHAT? Are you trying to tell me you never heard it?

24th April 2013

Me and Cookie are going to hypnotherapy on Sunday. The vetandhairyman said swimming will be good for me leg. Ha-ha, Cookie, I'm gonna duck ya... Let's see how your hair looks then, show girl.

Never trust girls. Me and Cookie were having some play time. Mum, Dad and Poobag were watching us to make sure we didn't get too rough. Cookie went inside to play with her toys and was really quiet. All of a sudden, she ran full speed and dived at me with a big growly roar. I was off balance, that's the only reason I fell on me bum, you big furball. I wasn't scared.

Cookie went to the vetandhairyman today to get worms. She had to go on the scaley things and they are new talking ones... They just sighed.

She weighs 36 of the killer-prams, and she is only a pupster. I hope she stops jumping on me sometime soon.

27th April 2013

Just for the hoomans that don't speak fluent anti-social media doglet, here are a few for you:

BOL – bark out loud
RORB – roll on rug barking
RORBFAO – as above whilst barking my furry ass off
HOL – howling out loud (it's funnier than barking out loud)
WTF – where's the food?
WYB – where you been?
WYBAD – where you been all day?
WOF – wee on floor (because of funny joke or, in the case of Spangles, just pleased to see you)
CCUB – cry constantly under breath (that's Spangle for, 'I'm excited ... excited ... EXCITED ... EXXCCIITTEEDD!'

We have others but they are classified. I could tell you them, but then I'd have to slobber on you.

28th April 2013

Off for a swim today with Princess Cookie. No number ones or number twos in the pool. No splashing, bombing or trying to drown your annoying little sister. Well, that sounds rubbish to me.

Just got back from hydro-ferry-pee. Cookie thought her name had changed to Jesus and she could walk on water. Straight in she went, as soon as she was off her lead – straight to the bottom like a big hairy brick. What could I do? Super Monty Dogge to the rescue, ta-da. In I went to rescue her big furry bum. Sisters – they're hard work.

1st May 2013

It's Cookie's first time at the beach today. The hoomanoids wonder what she'll think of it. Simple: she'll try to eat the sand and drink the water – this is COOKIE after all. If the swimming pool is anything to go by, she should be getting into Dublin about lunchtime. I'm not saving her again. I'm already regretting the first time.

6th May 2013

Mum and Dad let me and Cookie play last night 'cos they thought me leg was much better. Great, I had that flippin hairy hippo bouncing on me head. I think I'll limp again today.

Wow, it's sunny today. I saw lots of doggies I've never seen before on me walk . I wonder where they've been all winter.

Cookie got very friendly with a lady on her walk. Dad said they looked like they wus dancing. I think only one of them seemed to be enjoying it, though. And they say I'm the norty one.

> Unlike Monty, Cookie was a natural at swimming; the problem was trying to keep her out of the water so Monty could have a peaceful swim.

8th May 2013

Can someone rehome this flippin' sister of mine? I go swimming and she barks and barks and yelps until she can come in too. Then when she's in, she wants me toy – not hers, MINE!

I had to tow her back in, clinging to me dummy 'cos she wouldn't let go. She can properly swim now so it's all downhill for me.

Free to good home, frizzy dog with no manners, no social skills, permanent shoelaces and an appetite that makes a baby elephant seem picky. In fact, forget the good home, just any home pleeeeeaaaassseee...

9th May 2013

Saw some fishymen in the woods today. They were just coming back with their bags and stuff. I think they were called Rod – both of them. Dad said they'd been out all night. They sit there for hours till they catch the fish with their long sticks, then they put them back.

I think he's winding me up – even hoomans wouldn't be that silly. I didn't like 'em, anyhow. There was summat fishy about em. I gave 'em the Monty big woof but they still wanted to fuss me, so we made friends. I'm cheap, me.

> It's fair to say that Wigan winning the FA Cup Final caused a fair bit of excitement in the town but obviously not anything the dogs (and Monty, in particular) could understand.

11th May 2013

I live in Wigwam. Jeez, what is all the screaming about? Did someone put Quorn in the pies or summat? Dad says it's footyball and every dog has its day. I hope it's mine tomorrow.

Seriously though, I've not seen this much excitement here since they changed the benefit rules and stopped people claiming disability for wearing clogs.

12th May 2013

Mum and Dad found a white dove that couldn't fly, so they put it in the avietree so it could rest. It ate lots of food and got strong again. Now it's flying round the garden and I'm helping. I wait below to play with it when it lands. Funnily enough, it's flying really well and not landing at all now.

CHAPTER 9
Give Paw

> Newfoundlands are very vocal dogs. It can take a bit of getting used to, particularly if you don't know the breed. It's not surprising that not everybody 'gets it' when a thirteen-stone (180 lb) dog is barking at them because they want to say hello.

22nd May 2013

Me walk today:

- Met three people who gave me treats. That was good.
- Two people who just gave me fusses. That was OK.
- Five dogs who didn't want to play. Dull.
- One fisherman on a bike who went white when I barked at him. Priceless.

With me being not too well, Dad has been saying he wants the old Monty back. Well, your wish is my command.

I lay outside, you get cold and shut the door. I want to come in, you get up and open the door. I get warm and want to go outside, you get up and open the door. Repeat until you say you're sick of the old Monty and can I make my bl***y mind up.

Old Monty back in da house. And then out again. He-he.

23rd May 2013

Went for a walk over on the green tonight with the brown one. The hoomans are letting us play again 'cos me leg is better. Cookie is getting big now but she still rolls over when Monty Dogge nudges her at full Newfydoof speed. Mwah-ha-ha-ha.

I am feeling almost back to my normal self. I'm sure she can roll further, though. Must try harder

24th May 2013

There is a Jacky Rustle who chases the Spangles every time he sees 'em. He growls, barks and chases them 'cos they are scaredy cats. Today I saw him and I did the same to him. The scruffy little bully pooed himself.

Dad couldn't work out how I knew 'cos I'd never seen him be nasty to the dangly-eared ones. But I know, Dad ... I just know.

25th May 2013

Yesterday on me walk, I saw a man who always gives me a treat. I went straight over to him and gave him a little nudge just to remind him. He said I was really clever for remembering. Please: you give me a treat every time I see you, so what's clever about remembering that? Dad manages to remember where he lives most days, and my brain is much bigger than his.

Sunny day, off for a walk soon to the nature reserve then I'm going into town to meet me public. It's a tough life being me. I think sometimes I have more fans than Wigwam — actually, Bailey has more fans than Wigwam.

26th May 2013

Big day in Wigwam town centre today. People queued to have their photo taken with a national treasure. Anyway, enough about me – the FA cup was there, too.

27th May 2013

Saw Charlie, a friend of mine, on me walk today. He's a Cockypoobum and he's quick. I thought I had him, though. Full speed, wind behind me, and then he turned and went the other way. I just happened to be on the gravelly path at the time, and me legs wouldn't do what they were told. I disappeared in a cloud of dust and got a mouthful of stones.

Next time, Charlie boy, next time...

29th May 2013

With all the rain yesterday, it felt like we was in the sorry-tree confineyment. The hoomans don't do so well in the wet so I try to keep them dry. Looking forward to some adventures today. Not sure what, but I try to make every day an adventure.

Just been to town and met lots and lots of hoomans. I met a coote licckle Labbyrador who was only four mumfs old. He kept kissing me. We was playing so long that Dad was late getting back to the car and he got a letter from a nice man with a hat on called a trafficky war-down. Dad called him another name but I don't think that was his real name 'cos Dad said it under his breath.

Dad says I owe him twenty-five kwids. He makes me laff with his jokes.

30th May 2013

Dad just walked me and Cookie together. You may be surprised that we all got home in one piece. He neghostalated other dogs, a motorbike and two lorry things. He even picked up a poo in the bag, none on his hands, from the middle of the road.

This hooman training is going well. We may be able to keep him after all.

1st June 2013

Me and Cookie Bear went to the woods this morning. I managed to roll her into a fence post but she got me back and knocked me over when I weren't looking. 1–1 this time, but Cookie scored more for artyistick impression.

Just slobbered all over a Porche. Dad was impressed; he said I'd finally got some class. Now if that had been that pretty little whymyarmour I've had me eye on, that would have been class.

2nd June 2013

What's happening today then? Well, it's a walk in the naturist reserve to start off and then a little trip to Trebaron Garden Centre to see me friends. Then I think we're getting the paddling pool out ... wahayyy. I love playing dunk the Cookie, but she is getting big now so maybe we should play dunk the Bailey instead. He-he.

Dad's always saying he's happy as Larry and that I have the life of Riley, so somewhere there is a really, really happy bloke called Larry Riley.

Mum cooked new biccys yesterday and we had them on the walk today. Recall 100%. Slobbering 100%. Generally being a hooligan, always 100%.

3rd June 2013

Me and Cookie are off to the beach this morning. Don't worry if there are reports of a walrus seen on the beach at Formby, it'll just be the hooge brown beast or Dad. Both have similarities.

If you go down to the beach today...

4th June 2013

Lots of dogs on me walk today, never seen most of 'em before. Dad says they are special hibey-netting dogs that only come out when it's warm and sunny. Dad says the hibey-netting dogs are sometimes for old or poorly hoomans, but mainly for the ones that have the serious idleitis illness. I'm glad Dad only has the stoopid-idiot disease.

Just popped up to Saneysberries and waited outside with Dad. A nice lady with a bag of scrummy smelling food came to say hello. I'm sure she said give paw, honest. So, I did.

Those thin orange bags fall apart really easy, don't they? I only touched it gently. Nice of her to put all of her food on the floor for me. Dad wouldn't let me eat one bit, not even the packet of meat. How nasty is he?

Playing in the paddling pool with Cookie Bear today. She got a time out 'cos she's crazy. OK, I was teasing her a bit with the toys but you need to learn some self-control, ya licckle brown hooligan.

Mum and Dad said they're taking me to the Snake District on Friday. I'm not sure I like snakes, although I'm not absolutely serpent. That was a joke ... did ya get it? I crack meself up sometimes. I really am going there, though.

6th June 2013

Very hot today in Wigano del Sol. It's an early morning walk for me followed by a day in my room with the fan on, or I may wander out onto the patio to take in the breeze across the lake.

I do prefer going all-inclusive as I never have to carry cash ... such a drag. The service is OK but sometimes a little slow, and the staff don't always have good manners, but it will do. It was mentioned the other day that I was spoilt. Moi?

Cookie Bear is going to her very first show soon in Blackypool, aw, bless. Well good luck to the judge. First he's got to find out which end is which; both of them are always wet ... yuck.

Poobag is showing her, getting her to run without jumping all over the place, and then ... and then ... standing still ... rofbmfao.

I am going to watch. I can already feel the tears running down my legs.

7th June 2013

Me day trip has been cancelled 'cos Cookie Bear has got a poorly tummy and Mum and Dad won't leave her. She was spending the day with Poobag, but everyone is fussing round her now. I don't mind really, I just want me wrestling buddy to get well soon. I'm kinda getting used to her.

8th June 2013

Cookie Bear has a poorly tummy so, to make herself feel better, she decided to chew the rugs. Dad said he felt like he was picking a floating jigsaw up this morning … nice!

Mum and Dad play this silly game every evening. It's called wait-till-Monty-is-asleep-and-then-sneak-an-icecream. You think you're so clever but I nearly caught you last night, so tonight be afraid … be very afraid 'cos Monty is on to you, sneaky hoomans.

9th June 2013

Cookie Bear cracks me up. She went bombing through the undergrowth and picked up lots of sticky bits on her fur. Note to Cookie: don't try to remove a piece of bramble on the leg that you're just about to land on while running at full speed. Ouch – gravel rash on your nose has gotta hurt. No brown jokes from me though…

10th June 2013

Cookie Bear seems better today, so she'll mainly be annoying me. Still, at least the hoomans can stop fussing over her and get back to fussing over me. The mini-hoomans spent all weak-end in the paddling pool and they wouldn't let me in theirs 'cos there was a palm tree and giraffe thing on the side of it and they said I'd reck it. Me? I'm hurt, I really am.

Anyway, glad I didn't go in 'cos, by the look of that water it turned into a piddling pool.

I like going for walks after the hoomans have been out pit-nicking. This morning I found a strawberry milkshake from Macdougalls. There was still half left. I took it over to show Dad but by the time I got there it was all gone... Strange that.

11th June 2013

I have to sit by the front door in the morning 'cos waiting for the postyman is me main job during the day. I have to see if I can make him change from a pink colour to white. I do this by jumping up on me back legs and barking really loud at the top of me voice. He loves our game ... I fink.

The postyman just bought a letter and I am very excited. It's a pass for the doggy show in Blackypool and it's got my name on it. Dad said I'm in a special class NFC. He says it means 'no flippin' chance'. He says it's like football and some people are really good players and they play, and all the others go and watch. He says I'll be good at watching... Oh well, it's a day out, I suppose.

13th June 2013

Just been snapped at, growled at and barked at by a Yorkshire Pudding Terror. What did I do? I rose above it, ignored him and walked on. I saw him again further on me walk; same again. What did I do? I went for the little hooligan. He needs to learn some manners. His hoomans went a funny colour. Serve 'em right – teach him how to behave, stoopid peoples.

Mum's cooking chicken jerky. Do you know how lovely that smells? It's driving me cwazy. Is it ready yet?... Is it ready yet?... Is it ready yet?... Is it ready yet?... Is it ready yet?... Is it ready yet?... Is it ready yet?... Is it ready yet?... Is it ready yet?... Is it ready yet?

17th June 2013

Had a walk and behaved meself this morning. Got told off yesterday for being grumpy (OK, very grumpy) with another dog and had to stay on my lead all the way round. This morning I was like a little angel and got treats as well. Which Monty will Dad take out tomorrow? Now that would be telling.

19th June 2013

On me walk today I met a Snotwhiler and Dog-that's-bored-now. Well, I did me very best Monty-run-at-full speed, three bounces and land right in front of 'em. You know what? They weren't impressed, never cracked a smile ... didn't want to play or nuffin. Some doglets, just no sense of houmous.

Dad told me them Snotwhilers used to have no tails. The pupsters used to lose 'em in mummy's tummy. Now they give the mum supeyglue and bingo they come out with tails. I love Dad, he knows everyfink. He's like a cyclepedia.

20th June 2013

Saw a hooman today by the woods, he was just standing there looking at the trees. He had a cammyra thing, seen one of them, Mum is always pointing it at us. He had a funny thing too which went on his eyes. Dad said they were nockylarrs and they made things look bigger. Hoomans, hoomans, hoomans do you know nuffin? You just walk closer and then things look bigger... Tis easy.

He had no dog with him, no treats (checked his pockets twice) and he was holding the nockylar fings so he couldn't fuss me. The hooman was no use at all to me so I left.

21st June 2013

Me and Dad have been working on giving treats. Here's how it goes. I have a grumble at a dog as we pass. Dad says norty boy, leave. No treat. We walk past a dog, I just look at Dad with puppy-dog eyes, good boy. Treat. We repeat until we get to the point when the treat stops and I just get a good boy. I remind him how it goes; I grumble at the next dog. Norty boy, leave. No treat. Then we get back to treats when I leave. He is getting it but, boy, it's hard work.

Cookie Bear went into town today for sociallising. Twelve people thought she was a bear, six thought a Burnt Knees Mounting dog, four thought a St Bernarsey, and two said she was a Newfydoof. None guessed correctly that she is in fact a hippo wearing a hairy rug from Ikea.

22nd June 2013

It appears Cookie Bear is having a pampering day to try to make her look beautiful. The show is tomorrow. Hoomans, you need a miracle, not a day.

Hoomans are off shopping. I'm going to keep an eye on Dad while he loiters around outside chatting to anyone who'll listen. It's some life, this. I thought I had such a bright future when I was a pup.

I think I need to join a union – can anybody help? I'm pretty sure Dad was running a child-minding service in the foyer at Sainysberries. I was the only member of staff and the ratio children to Newfs seemed a bit high. I think I'm being exploitalated.

23rd June 2013

Been to Blackypool today to the dog show. Cookie Bear walked round a bit, had a little run, let that fella feel her bum and then got a tiffycate. Everyone was saying well done and stuff. Easy peasey orange weezy, if you ask me.

I had great fun, though. I met lots of luvvly hoomans and some real grumpy ones too. Met some lovely doggies and some real grumpy ones, too. It's funny the grumpy hoomans were with the grumpy dogs. Dad says they had something up their bum. I wonder what.

24th June 2013

Well today has been a bit of an anti-climax. I had breakfast, a couple of walks, dinner and a couple of poos. Add a bit of TV, a job, and I could be a hooman.

CHAPTER 10
Maybe They're Breakfast

25th June 2013

Met Bella the Snotwhiler this morning in the woods. We played a bit together so I think I'm growing on her. Her brother the Dog-that's-bored-now is a bit grumpy, though. Mind you, I think I would be if I had wrinkles like that.

26th June 2013

Off into town this morning to suppeyvise Dad while the lady hoomans go shopping. I wish he would learn that when the ladies say, 'Oh look at him, he's gorgyoos,' he doesn't need to turn round. They're not talking about him. On the other paw, if people say, 'Look at him, he's a big boy,' they may be talking about him, just not in the way he thinks they are. Poor, poor hooman dad.

Me and the Spangles rolled in a new smell today. When we came back Mum said, 'It's hooman poo, Jesus Christ.' Not sure who he is, but if Mum gets hold of him he's in trouble.

Dad said it's what the lazy fishhymen do. I think he means it's the lazy fishhymen's doo.

28th June 2013

Dad says he despairs of me. I think that's another word for proud, int'it?

I had fun at the shops today. I gave lots of fusses and kisses to peoples and had photos and then I smelt something dillyicious. It was coming from a lady's little trolley thingy so I jumped up to have a look. Well, I sort of got me head stuck in the bag, and me front legs stuck in the trolley and then it just started moving. Dad let go of me lead cos he said I was going to decapsalate an old lady. Me steering was rubbish 'cos me head was in the bag but I nearly made it through the door.

The next thing I know, Dad is wrestling me head out the bag like a crazy hooman. He's such a spoilsport. I nearly had it. The lady was very nice, she said I had good taste. It was ribeye snake ... so close but oh so far.

29th June 2013

Going into town 'cos its Armed Forces Day. I hope they'll let me play with some guns, bang bang. Or maybe they'll let me throw some of them grenaidey things, whoooosssshh, bang. I can't wait.

Had a great time at the parade but I am really tired now. When all the soldiers marched past everyone started clapping. I find clapping really hard so I just barked really loud until they went past. Some people jumped but most of them smiled. It was great fun. Dad was talking to some of those vetyruns, they was very brave. I don't think I could be that brave, but maybe if there was a war I could bark and make the baddies jump.

30th June 2013

Off to a car boot sale this morning. Dad says I have a special job. I have to get as many peoples round as possible so they can sell them all their rubbish. It seems easy enough. He says I'm on con-mission. The more people come, the more biccies I get. It sounds like my kind of work.

When we get back, it's Molly Spangle's birthday party. Mum has baked a cake and says she is going to get a picture of all five of us sitting nicely with party hats on. Dad says he'd bet anything that that ain't gonna happen. For the first time in my life, I think Dad is right.

Look who lost her hat...obviously

21st July 2013

Mum and Dad have been really busy lately and Dad hasn't been able to help me type, so I haven't been on Farcebook much. I tried to get Bailey to help as he has small paws. Unfortunately, small paws comes with a small brain so that was useless. Have no fear, hoomans, I am back. Some fwends have said they missed me funny comments so here goes ... ummm ... ummm ... I'll fink of summat soon... OK, OK. What do you call a clever Cockeyed Spangle? If you can find one, I'll let you know.

22nd July 2013

It is cooler today in Wigwam, so me and the Cookster went for a walk this morning down the canal. I saw some Spangles and never jumped on 'em, so points for me there... This afternoon I went to Saneysberries and Cookie went to somewhere called Go Indoors. I was perfect and met lots of hooman fwends, didn't mug anyone for food or frighten any old ladies. More points. Cookie Bear managed to slobber all over the expensive clothes, knock a display over and eat all the biscuits left out for the doggies. Ha-ha... Who's a good boy then? Bad, bad puppy.

23rd July 2013

Just been for me walk down the canal. There was a really long thin boat tied up on the side, so I thought I might go in and have a look around. Dad said you can't just go in, and besides they are having their breakfast. Then their dogs came to tell me off. There was three of them, they were really long and had little tiny legs. They must be special dogs made to fit on those boats. Dad said they were sausage dogs. Mmm, maybe they were breakfast.

24th July 2013

Dad said I nearly committed treacle today, or summat like that. I said a funny comment about the royal family and he told me I shouldn't. He said if you do the treacle you get locked up in the tower of Londinium. He says they get Newfydoofs and chain them up. Then they punish them by making them listen to special recordings of Spangles whining all daaaayyy long. Ah, just like being at home, then.

Dad just took Cookie Bear into town for a meet and greet and to introduce the people of Wigwam to some extra-long slobbering laces. Two drunk blokes were a bit rowdy and when they saw Cookie this was the conversation.

Drunk... 'Hey mate is that a bleeding bear?'
Dad... 'Do you think it is?'
Drunk... 'Yeah.'
Dad... 'It is then.'
Drunk... 'You think you're bleeding clever?'
Dad... 'Just above average, if I had to guess.'
Drunk... 'Well you're not, you're stupid, mate.'
Dad... 'That's as maybe but I've never mistaken a dog for a bear before...'
Drunk's mate dragged him away ... luckily.

25th July 2013

Just laying out on the patio and rolled over onto me back, as you do. Just at that moment a women four houses up shouted, 'It's a boy.' Now I know I'm a rather large lad, but that is very good eyes from that distance.

I ain't going anywhere in this storm. It's scary. Maybe for fun later we can tie Bailey to the rotary line and see if the lightning can restart his brain.

26th July 2013

I've been down to the shops this afternoon while Mum and Dad went shopping. Dad took me into Pets-All-You-Can-Eat-Before-They-Catch-You while Mum went into mum-type shops. I met some nice hoomans who gave me lots of fusses. They were with a man called Graham, he was in a wheelychair and loved dogs. They said he couldn't move at all. I helped him find all the pie he'd dropped. I could be one of those helping dogs. I could do that every day.

Does anyone else get so distracted by sniffing that they walk into things? You know – cars, walls, lamp posts, gates? Tonight was a Vocksall Zofearer... Ouch

I love an all you can eat buffet

27th July 2013

Every time I meet Daisy the chocolate Labratorydor she runs up to me wagging her whole body. Then she shoves her bum in me face and licks me mouth for ages. Dad says she lurrrrvs me. How do you tell a girl we can only ever be fwends?

28th July 2013

Me and Cookie Bear are out first this morning due to the heat. Why are we always second, you may ask? Well that is because the Spangles whinge and whine from first thing in the morning till they get out. Dad's answer? Take them out first. What lessons do they learn? Good parenting there, Dad. See what I have to live with?

30th July 2013

We had a ternative dog show here this weekend 'cos we feel left out. Dog shows have some funny cattygorries, like post-graduate dog. I mean, have you ever met a dog with a master's degree? We picked some cattygorries we could win. Some winners were obvious but where there was an argument the hoomans decidled.

Pretty show girl looks...
1. Cookie Bear
Close second Bailey

Best fluttery eyelashes
1. Bailey

Poo eater (all varieties)
1. Poppy ... only one entry

Bogoff expert
1. Molly

Best chaser (cars, buses, pigeons, dustmen ... everything)
1. Monty

Lives for water
1. Molly
Cookie very close second

Slobber (all cattygories ... length, amount, stickiness)
1. Cookie ... no contest

Whiner (all cattygories ... pitch, length of whine, amount per day)
1. Bailey ... no contest

What happened next? (most unpredickteeball)
1. Monty ... no contest

Most intelligent (we asked Dad to decide but he didn't understand the question)
In reverse order

3. Browns

2. Black...

1. White and another colour... I didn't want to upset them and I know they won't understand heheheh

I think we all qualified for Crufties.

Been down the canal and the field this morning on me walk. Met loads of doggie fwends. Was playing with Sam Oyed ... funny name, ain't it? I think he used to look like me but lost his black bits. It's OK, rolled around with him for a bit and he's got them back now. I'm just happy to help.

5ᵗʰ August 2013

Cool and wet. Ahhhh, heaven. I have spent weeks laying around under me fan or in the paddling pool, not a bad life but gets a bit boring. I am definitely a winter dog while Dad is a summer hooman. Ah well, as the saying goes, you say tomayto I say – why you talking like an American?

Cookie Bear is being nortier than a norty dog on National Norty Dog day. She is running round like a lunartick and chewing things up. Dad says it's her hore-moans. I'm not sure what he means but I wish her hores would stop moaning soon.

CHAPTER 11
Peas, Chips And Gravy

6th August 2013

We were crossing a road this morning and this very nice hooman in a car stopped to let us cross. Dad waved to him to thank him just at the point I needed to go, you know ... number twos. Dad went all stroppy and said I was holding all the traffic up. The hoomans didn't mind. They were just laffing.

Had enough of Cookie Bear today. She never stops jumping on me, wanting to play. I had to go under the bench so she couldn't get me. Dad called me a big wuss... What's one of them, then?

7th August 2013

Well, that was a fun walk. It was about as dull as the water you find in the dishes. Met a Staffie who wanted to fight me, and a dog who wouldn't even look at me and walked past really fast. There was a riot of Spangles across the canal and I couldn't go and play. So all in all, pretty boring. If it hadn't been for the hooge amounts of goose poo it would have been a right off.

8th August 2013

Mum has started brushing me at night about half past eight. This is not fair as I know she is doing it, but I am powerless to fidget or run away. It's like she has put a big invissybull straight jacket on me. See what I have to live with? Sneaky, sneaky hoomans.

Better walk today. We went over the canal and I met the Spangles, two Jack Rustly terrors and an English Settee. Nobody wanted to play but I got some fusses. On the way back met Oscar the Springy Spangle and his mum, who gives me treats. After that Dad had a row with a lorry driver who nearly ran us over. Normal service resumed... Well, everyone has to have hobbies.

9th August 2013

I just had a dog have a proper go at me. Dad said it was real shocker that the dog was so aggressive, especially as the owner seemed very relaxed sitting outside Tesco drinking his cider. Even Dad don't start on the wobbly-leg-water that early.

It's four weeks today till Mum and Dad go on their snollydays. Dad was telling me about it today. It's a very dangerous place where you could get attacked at any time. A lot of the children don't go to school and there isn't always electricity and clean water. I'm not entirely comfortable about them stopping in Coventry.

12th August 2013

Hmmm someone's in the bad books. They sneaked into the kitchen and ate all the paella. I'll give you one guess and I'll give you a clue: it wasn't me or a Spangle.

14th August 2013

When I was walking down the canal this morning, there was a Laberadoor swimming. It had a bottle and ball and was trying to get them both. It got the bottle ... left it ... got the ball ... left it. Ha-ha, it was there for ages. Guess what colour it was? Yep ... brown.

15ᵗʰ August 2013

Bailey has to go in for a hoppyration today. He has something wrong with his lips and he has to have drastic surgery. On the letter from the vetandhairyman it says, 'While Bailey is under GA it is a good time to get those other little proseedurrs done like teeth cleaning.' How about ear shortening or brain detection? That would useful. Only joking Bails, good luck me licckle arch-enema.

18ᵗʰ August 2013

Off on a trip with Dad this morning. He hasn't told me where; he says it's a surprise. Now what does that mean? Road trips with Dad are always, erm, interesting. We always get lost, and nearly always muddy and wet, and that's just Dad.

Been for a drive and then a walk down the canal. Made some new friends and barked at some boats. Saw a man on a bike.

Monty, good boy ... leave ... leeaavve ... leeeevvvveee ... leeeeeeeeeevvvvvvvveeeeee... Nah, just had to have a jump at him. Wobbly bike, very funny. Well, for me it was. Dad wasn't impressed.

19ᵗʰ August 2013

Two dogs on me walk. I wanted to play but missed the first one. Second one went to walk past so I did me bestest jump in the air and land in front of her, wagging me tail with me bum in air. I didn't know she was deaf and nearly blind. Whoops. It scared her and she ran into the reeds, then she got in a panic and ran the wrong way towards the lake. Dad helped and they got her back about twenty minutes later. Bad, boy Monty. I didn't mean it ... honest.

21st August 2013

Happy birthday, Mum. I hope you get loads of pressies, you deserve them for putting up with Dad. All of us are going to be really good today. Well, most of us anyway... Well, the Spangles are... Well, Molly said she'd be good this morning ... that's our pressie ... have a great day.

22nd August 2013

There were fishymen down the bottom of the garden last night. They have been there before, leaving rubbish and old hooks everywhere, so Mum asked them to leave. I barked as loud as I could till they did. I even scared meself a bit.

24th August 2013

Been out for a walk with Cookie Bear and now I'm going out with Mum and Dad to a place called Cheshire Oaks. Sounds like a big forest somewhere. I should be able to wee up lots of trees. Nah it had lots of shops. You can wee up those though, so it was still fun.

25th August 2013

So Cookie Bear gets a trip out with Dad to Rivington. She went swimming in the ressyvoyeur, met lots of doggies and played in the woods. Where did I go? Saneysberries... Cheers, Dad.

26th August 2013

Off to the fun day today with Dad. It says there are stalls, the fire brigade will be there and lots of other attractions, which all sound very boring. But I was interested in face painting. I'm thinking a tiger – what do you think?

There is also a bouncy castle and barbeque. Mini-hoomans jumping up and down with food in their hands seems too good an opportunity to miss.

Cookie just weed in the paddling pool then dropped her teddy in there. Girls are disgusting.

27th August 2013

Met a choccylate Laberadoor this morning. She was a young one and ran up to me, jumping all over me, barking and snapping at my face. Her mum said she's a really norty girl and it's amazing that I stand for it. I live with Cookie, so honestly it was nothing. I hardly knew she was there.

I was asleep outside last night, dreaming I'd just grown wings and was about to catch me some pigeons, when Poobag woke me up calling my name. Now that only means two things: a treat, or time to come in. I opened one eye and saw something in her hand. I was excited and ran in really fast for a ... minty Dentastick!!! Have you ever had one of them? Corrugated cardboard dipped in toothpaste would taste better. Yuck, yuck, yuck. Still ate it though, and then gave Dad loads of sloppy kisses ... mmm, minty fresh.

A year of planning and we were ready. To celebrate our thirtieth wedding anniversary we were going on our dream holiday to Kenya on safari. This meant Emma was looking after the dogs. But was she in charge?

6th September 2013

Well, Mum and Dad have been putting fings into bags for days now. I knew something was up and now I know. They are going on their snollydays today. I won't see them for two weeks. Guess I'm in charge then ... hmmm, could be fun.

8th September 2013

Mum and Dad have been gone on their snollydays a few days ago now and Mummy Poobag is looking after me. She is spending a lot of time with me – something about missing Mum and Dad? I think she might be missing them, or missing a bit of help around the house more like. I have been really good (as I usually am) and I am making sure I behave as good with Mummy Poobag as I do with Mum and Dad.

My check list is going well.

> Poo in the road a lot – CHECK
> Bark at the fishymen loudly – CHECK
> Minty breath kisses after Dentastix – CHECK

I surprise myself sometimes just how thoughtful I am.

9th September 2013

Just had a message from Dad. He said, 'Monty, hope you're being a good boy. We have found something bigger than you and much better behaved. It only chews the things it's supposed to and doesn't need brushing every hour. We may bring him back and swap... Love Dad xxx'.

See what I have to put up with? He's in another incontinent and he's still sarcaustic.

25ᵗʰ September 2013

Well Mum and Dad are back from snollydays, and guess what? No pressie for me. Mum said they didn't see anything they could bring me back, but they have adopted two elephants. She said me and Cookie could be redundyant as the two big, clumsy house pets.

26ᵗʰ September 2013

Glad Dad's back because me and Cookie can walk together. Not that I like walking with Miss Piddlepants. It's just that she is much nortyerer than me, so I can get away with more. Not just a pretty face, me.

28ᵗʰ September 2013

Been waiting all week for the elephants to turn up, only to find out they're not coming. Dad says they have adopted them but they just send money to help feed and look after them —they don't live with us. He said it's a great idea and he was thinking of doing the same with me and Cookie Bear. See. He's back five minutes and he's already being nasty to me.

29ᵗʰ September 2013

Mum and Poobag have been to the warehouse. While they were there, Dad took me for a walk down the canal. Dad likes that walk 'cos there are lots of places to stop. They're called pubs. We sat outside and I helped Dad eat his sarnie, but he said I couldn't have any beer 'cos I'm rowdy enuff already.

I met lots of people and two little girls wanted to fuss me and have kisses. They said they had three dogs called Peas, Chips and Gravy... Only in Wigwam.

4th October 2013

Just been up to the learning zoo to help fetch the mini-hoomans. I've not been up for a long time and everyone came up for cuddles. There were some new extra mini-hoomans I'd not seen before, and they all wanted to say hello. I gave them lots of Monty-kissy-slobber for their new ooniforms. well, it's Friday so they need washing anyways.

CHAPTER 12
Can I Rescue Your Toy?

Oh no! I just found out yesterday was National Poetry Day.
I missed it. I lurv poetry. It's not too late to show you one
of mine is it?

> This life we live is but a journey,
> Some bits are sad and some are fourney.
> Be nice to peoples that you meet
> And in the end all will be reet...
> What do you fink ,peoples?

5th October 2013

Been out on a little tour this afternoon. Cookie has a dodgy
tummy, so she stopped at home to poo. We went to the
shopping centre. Pets at Home was full of Greathounds.
They were collecting for something – maybe a proper waist
because they are very thin.

Then we went past Maccydougals and there were loads
of hoomans sitting outside who wanted kisses. The people
who worked there came out and said if we sat down, they
would bring me some food. Dad said no 'cos we're watching
our waistlines. Maybe we should have gone and got the
Greathounds... They were looking for theirs.

6th October 2013

Dad said I am now very socialised. He said that a man
could run up to me dressed as a nun singing the national

anthem while swinging a baby around his head and I wouldn't react. Yeah right, where would that happen? Ooh, I forgot — I live in Wigwam.

7th October

Cookie was sick today and then had the runny-bum-sqwibby-pant thing. What did she have for tea? Chicken with pumpkin topped with a goat's milk yoghurt sauce. What did I have? That'll be the usual then ... notjealousatall.com

Awww, Cookie Bear gave Mummy and Daddy a icckle pwesent, a Sunday morning vet visit. £120 whoooosh gone... She is very generous that girl.

8th October 2013

Been for a walk tonight on me own 'cos Cookie was still practising solid poos. Off me lead all the way, met a few ickle dogs and said hello. I was very well behaved. Then we met a dog on a lead that was proppa nutty, goin for me and everyfink. He was like a devil-dog. Dad called me back but my recall needs some work. There, I said it. The truth that you all know. My hoomans are rubbish at the trainin' stuff.

In the end Dad really shouted like he was meaning it, so I came back. They said I was a good boy, so mission acumpylished. Monty out... Over.

9th October 2013

Just been for a little road walk. As we go down the streets, all the dogs in the houses and back gardens bark at me. Some go crazy, really crazy, spinning round in circles and jumping up and down growling and barking. With those I am very quiet and calmly wee up their gate post. Let's see you get one higher than that next time you're out... Is that mean?

> We had been contacted by the Newfoundland Club and asked if we could make Monty's little stories official and do them under the club banner. Life According to Monty Dogge was official. Though the club link was short-lived due to personalities getting in the way, the ramblings continue to this day.

10th October 2013

I always knew I'd be famous one day. Dad always thought it would be for holding up the traffic in Wigwam town centre while I had a poo, but he has no faith in me. The Newfoundland Club have asked me to do a blob. I know I have to hexplain stuff to you hoomans, so that's where I have to write something every day and give hoomans and doglets advice about stuff. Sounds easy enough to me so I've started. You can find me at Life According to Monty Dogge ... that's me page.

Got very excited last night and went to give Dad a big kiss. I forgot to put me tongue out though, and just ended up poking him in the face with me nose. His head made a funny noise when it hit the wall... Mum said it's the sound of something hollow hitting something hard.

12th October 2013

Yay ... off to the seaside tomorrow at Formby with Dad. Don't worry if you see a hooge creature running along the beach. I'll keep him under control.

*Don't scare the
locals Dad*

13th October 2013

Well, this is like day 1 in the Big Brother House. I have been
asked by the Newfoundland Club to jot down a few of my
thoughts about life on a daily basis. I will be able to give
advice on many things like training your hooman, and living
without testicles. I also have an assistant in the form of
Cookie Bear. Her role will mainly be looking pretty and drooling.
My hoomans will help – they find the keyboredy thing easier
to use with their hairless paws, and they like to feel useful
(something they aren't, but you'll soon realise that).

That's me, Monty Dogge signing off for tonight. Let's see
what tomorrow brings... And Cookie? She's asleep.

Thought you'd like to know that I am a propa water rescue
dog. Fearless, ready to go at a moment's notice and fully
trained to Level 1. This means I am fully qualified to rescue
a toy if it was to fall in the water. I patrol the lake and
canaly place just in case a toy should be drowning. Not found
one yet, but it must be nice for the people of Wigwam to
know that their toys are safe.

Toy rescuer
expert level

14th October 2013

I decided today was a good day to return to stealth poos.
Now kids, the trick is to pop out your number twos in
segments without breaking stride, like depth charges. I
used to do it all the time but Dad sussed me and it's no fun.
If you do it right, you can leave a trail about fifty yards
long and then your hooman realises they have to go all the
way back and pick 'em up. It's even more fun if they don't
notice and someone has to tell 'em. He-he, they go a funny
red colour. It's even more funny if they only have one poo
bag left and they have to try to get 'em all in. I know, I
know, it's juvenile and childish, but it's very funny and the
hoomans love licckle games like these.

15th October 2013

Well, it's the weak-end and I know you hoomans love having
the weak-end. It doesn't make much diffyrence to me really,
but I do get trips out on top of me walks. These are what

Dad calls our socialie-sation and they make us responsible members of society... Ha.

What it means is that Dad gets to sit outside the shop chatting while Mum gets all the food and does all the work. I do like meeting new people and making new four-legged friends, but the other dogs always ask the same questions time after time...

'Does he live in the house?' If Mum had her way no, and he has spent a few nights in the garden but that's a long story.

'Does he eat a lot?' DUH...look at him.

'I bet he needs a lot of exercise.' As previous question.

'Does he lose a lot of hair?' Yep, he says its stress, but we know it's the getting old thing.

'I bet he slobbers a lot.' When he drinks the falling over water he slobbers, snores and makes noises from his bum. Mum calls him an old dunk.

'Is he good with children?' He's OK, but I wouldn't leave him alone with them.

Hoomans are strange things, ain't they? The weak-end. I can't wait.

Dad says he wants to do some more training this weak-end. Yippee doo, hope it's with the Spangles...

> Despite turning two, Monty had still not turned into the calm and well- socialised dog he was to become. Added to this, we now had Cookie who was never destined to be calm. It kept us entertained and on our toes, that's for sure.

16th October 2013

Cookie went to see the vetandhairyman yesterday. Jumping up and knocking the leaflet display off the counter goes nowhere near my record, you licckle Brown pretender. I cleared the whole counter, including a vase of flowers, and still got a kiss from the deceptionist. You need to try harder, Cookster.

17th October 2013

Went for a walk tonight with Cookie. There was a mini-hooman over the road who was laffing and pointing as we walked past. His mum and dad asked if he could come and see us and he came over. After he had stroked us and had kisses, he said to his dad, 'I want to go and play big doggies.' His dad's face was a picture. Have fun with that, hooman parent.

18th October 2013

Me and the hairy hippo went to the shopping centre at the weekend for our socialie-station lessons. We went to a place called St Helens. It's funny 'cos we didn't see any saints and nobody was called Helen, but we made lots of new friendlies.

Dad was holding Cookie just on her lead and collar 'cos you know how he struggles to get her head collar on. A couple came over to fuss us and were saying how lovely we were. They said they had been looking to get a Newfydoof or Burnt Knees Mounting dog and didn't know which would suit them best, so they were asking Dad lots of questions.

Just then, the wind blew a big paper bag past Cookie. We like the moving paper bags, so off she went. Then it blew back, followed by Cookie, and then it went into the air and went off really fast the other way – and so did Cookie. Dad looked like one of them windmill things with a big shiny red face as he was trying to explain what it was like to live with the Newfydoofs... Ha-ha guess they'll be asking Bernie if they can have one of his mounting dogs.

19th October 2013

I think it's funny when me and Cookie are out and about in Wigwam and people ask our names. Dad says Monty and Cookie, and they're usually OK with my name but they have to translate her name into Wigwamese: 'Ello, Koookey.' If Dad's being sarcaustic he says, 'No, it's Cookie.' Then there's silence and a strange look. I fink it's what you hoomans call a bumbleweed moment. 'Argh, shiz luvleh, ain't ya, Koookey?'

20th October 2013

Cookie now goes up to the school with the mini-hoomans every morning and worryingly she is building her own little fan club. That is until this morning when she decided to play kiddie skittles. Cookie was getting lots of cuddles when she turned round fast and bumped a mini-hooman ... who bumped a mini-hooman ... who bumped a mini-hooman... Monty is officially favourite school dog again. Nice try, big brown buffoon.

21st October 2013

A bit windy on our walk tonight, and not just Dad for a change. I was behaving, minding my own busyness, then suddenly out of nowhere there's a piece of paper. Ooh, piece of paper, piece of paper... Got it... Oops, sorry Poobag, hope your leg is OK tomorrow.

Dad said when he took Cookie out this morning, she barked at a chap with a hood on who was revving his car and driving stoopid. Ah, that'll be her hooman-idiot radar coming through. Good girl.

22nd October

A bit concerned to tell you the truth. Dad took Cookie out last night for a walk to help her socialisey and get used to being out in the dark. Then I found out he took her to Southport for a walk along the seaside-front thingy. Then she went up to the school this morning and got a 10/10 in not knocking mini-hoomans over. She is becoming a daddy's girl...shouldIbeconcerned.com.

23rd October

Mum and Dad had to pop to the shops, so they took Cookie with them. On the way back to the car Cookie walked into five metal bollards in a row while she was trying to see what was going on behind her...bang...bang...bang...bang...bang...I'm waiting to see if it's knocked any sense into her... No.

25th October

It's raining really heavy and the Spangles won't go out to the toiletey. In half an hour Dad will take them out for a walk and they'll go crazy. They'll jump, splash and roll round in the puddles and the mud. Spangles... I rest my case your honour.

Now, busy weekend for me and the Brown Bomber. Today Cookie did meet and slobber in Wigwam town centre at the Dog's Trust stand. Tomorrow it's my turn to put a shift in and I'll be there all morning. Sunday we are going to a New castle. Not sure how new it is but it's Moby's birthday party and he's invited lots of peoples and doglets, fink there will be about a trillion Newfydoofs. Moby is Cookie's bruvver and she will meet her family again and there is talk of fish and chips. There may even be ice cream and if we're really lucky we can sneak off and leave her before anyone notices.

28th October 2013

We had a fantastic day yesterday up Newcastley. Met lots of other Newfydoofs, had a paddle in the sea and me and Woody managed to get some peace from annoying sisters. Cookie met her match yesterday with her sister Molly and I found that really funny. We had fish and chips in the car at the end, Buffday cake but no ice cream. Moby, Cookie's bro got sin-binned for getting too excited. It used to happen to me all the time big fella it's when your testyostyfoam starts coming through and makes you act like the hulk. Only downside was spending hours in the car with hairy hippo girl and she kept kissing me all the time...yuuuccckkkk.

When we were walking along the footpath at the beach yesterday a man asked if we could clear the path so his wife could pass as she was scared of dogs. He was very miseryable, Dad said some people should live in an airtight bubble. Hang on, Dad, surely then they wouldn't be able to brea... ahhh I get it.

30th October 2013

I have been in the car with Dad most of the day on our trip to Yorkshire Pudding Land. I have learnt some new words. He doesn't say them when mum's in the car.

31st October 2013

Dad walked Cookie off her head collar this morning as part of her training. It seems to be working, she has trained Dad to leave her head collar off most of the time. Dad said she was really good till she saw a young hooman bloke with a bag of food shopping. She lurched across really quickly and stuck her head in his bag. Dad said he's never seen anyone who has complete terror in their eyes, but their body is saying... 'I'm a cool dude... I'm a cool dude'... Ha-ha hoomans you do make me larf.

1st **November 2013**

Me and Cookie went trick or treating last night with the mini-hoomans. They knocked on the door and got sweets from the people inside. Hang on, they keep getting told not to talk to strangers but it seems OK if they give you sweets. You hoomans confoose me.

Well me and me silly brown sister got diddly snot... Nothing... Not a bean, no treats. I can't help thinking they took us as some sort of potential trick warning. Look what happens if they don't do the treat bit.

Surely if we were there as the heavies there is a minimum wage?

CHAPTER 13
The Newfydoof Poppy Seller

On a visit to our local supermarket I got chatting to Bob, a veteran who was collecting for the British Legion poppy appeal. As we spoke, more and more people came over to see Monty and bought a poppy. Bob joked that he had never taken so much money, and could we stay.

Monty and I did stay. In fact, Monty, Cookie and the family all took turns over the next four years to help.

What Monty started would see us help raise around £40,000 during that time – and he even got to meet the Lady Mayoress!

2nd November 2013

Could be another busy day for me. Dad says Cookie has lady things going on, so I have to do all the work by meself. I am out again helping the poppy hoomans. It's easy I just sit there, wag me tail, give em kisses, see if I can stick me head in their bag and find anything tasty, then they buy a poppy and it's on to the next one.

Tonight, I'm on barking at the fireworks duty. Dad says he wants it to rain all night. He usually doesn't like the rain but I stopped trying to work him out a long time ago... I'm clever but not that clever.

Just come back for me lunchybreak after giving out kisses, cuddles and poppies...whew we have been really busy with lots and lots of hoomans giving money. I have a fession to make. When the old Poppy soldier wasn't looking I drank his coffee. I know, I know but I think I'm adickid to it. Dad was talking to someone and when he looked round it had all gone, just slobber left. The soldier didn't mind he says he lurvs me and I can never be norty. That sounds like an invite to me.

Me soldier fwend must have forgiven me for drinking his coffee cos he wants me to walk with him at the front of the parade next Sunday in Wigwam. I don't usually worry about much but I am a bit nervous now. I will be really proud too so I'd better get a good brush and get Mum to wash me bib.

3rd November 2013

Day off today from my busy schedule. I've been for a walk and practised me stealth pooing for next Sunday (joking Dad, honest). May go down to the all you can eat buffet later, or Pets at Home as it's sometimes called.

There are some strange hoomans. Been out today and this lady was walking past with a mini-hooman... 'look at that big doggie... t'll eat ya rarrrrrr'. Now I'm no parenting expert but it seems a bit strange to me that you want to scare your children. If I had pups I couldn't imagine me pointing to a big fella come out of Maccydougals and saying 'look at him... you're next'

Strange hooman number 2... I was having fusses outside Pets-At-Fill-Your-Face-With-Their-Biscuits-And-Run when a woman pushed through and started rubbing me head.

Her: 'It's lovely, what make is it?'

Dad: 'HE'S a Newfoundland.'

Her: 'A what?'

Dad: 'He's a Newfoundland.'

Her: 'A what?'

Dad: 'He's a NEW-FOUND-LAND.'

Her: 'Never heard of it ... is it a dog?'

Dad: 'Seriously, are you for real?'

Her: Gone.

4th November 2013

Well it's a bit colder today... There was a frost and I was just thinking it'll be time soon for the Spangles to have their licckle, teeny, winter-drying coats on. Awww, bwess their icckle cotton socks.

Wow, this poppy-selling stuff is hard work. I've been up again today and I'm tired. The old soldier man is seventy-six and that is even older than Dad. Hard to believe, isn't it? When he was in the army he was a dog handle-her and had a dog called Colonel who sniffed out bombs and stuff. I think I'll stick to sniffing out chicken in hoomans' shopping bags, seems a bit safer. I did eat a poppy today. It wasn't very nice, but the old soldier said everyone should have a poppy so I thought I would.

5th November 2013

Dad says his broad bean wasn't working so he couldn't go on tinternet. We had our walk and food OK, so it's obviously nothing important. It must be just hooman whining stuff again.

Have I given some kisses out today? Six hours of duty, and lots of the poppies gone, and you know I never ate one. People are bringing me treats now 'cos I'm there every day. They say 'Awww, look at his sad eyes... I have to give him something.' I do sad eyes really well, it's me speccy-ally-tea.

Still can't believe that when the layydees say, 'Look at him, he's gawwjuss,' Dad still turns round. I do lurv his optynism. Give it up, Dad, there's only one bad boy them girls are talkin' 'bout.

6th November 2013

I love this time of the year. Hoomans spend all their time telling mini-hoomans not to talk to strangers and that there is no such thing as monsters. Then they send them out dressed as monsters to get sweets from strangers. Then they go and buy explosyives which cost a lot of money, and they set fire to them so they go bang, the louder the better. Then they go back to complayning about everyone who ever makes a noise. I lurv you hoomans. Next, it's Cwissymouse. I can hardly wait.

Our reaction to fireworks.

> Me: They are a bit annoying. I bark if a loud one goes off. After half an hour, I need to sleep.

> Molly: I have no feelings one way or the other. That would mean showing emotion.

Poppy: I'm terrified, it's the end of the world...
They're coming to get me. It's similar to my own
shadow, other dogs, people, bikes, bags, erm ...
everything really.

Cookie: Can I play with em? Go on, let me play
with em. When I jump, they go bang... Look, jump
– bang. Wheeeeee...

Bailey: What was the question?

Really not sure I'm cut out for this working lark. I've only
done a few days and I can't keep me eyes open. At least I
know now why you hoomans are so miserable, especially on
Mondays, Tuesdays, all of Wednesday, most of Thursday, and
Friday morning. Oh, and Sunday evening cos you're dreading
the work again. Ahh, it's a dog's life. Remind me again who
are the superior spee-cheese?

I'm on Twitter. Funny, that's what I thought people
called Dad when he was stoopider than yesterday. 'He was
a twit before, he's even Twitter today.' No, it's another
social meteor thingymajig. I am now officially a hashbag,
whatever that is ... #montydogge.

It's lovely to see so many ladies in Wigwam really making an
effort for Movember.

7th November 2013

Up at the Saneysberrys today and imagine my surprise when
another Newfydoof turned up. Not only that, but it was
a Land-spear like me and ... it was a girl. Wow, I thought
there is a DoGod. Dad took me outside to meet her. I gave
her the puppy dog eyes and me best bum waggle. She bit
me. OK, back to the snoring bored.

I remember the days when my Farcebook posties used to be funny about little things that happened to me on my walks or on little trips out. About pooing in the road, or being barked at by Shit-zoos. Now I just do the same thing day after day. Up early, rushed lunch break, home for dinner and then bed. You know what? I almost feel hooman.

8th November 2013

Me old soldier mate Bob used to do his soldiering stuff in the Irish Fuzzy-ears. I know soldiers is tuff but he wears a skirt. Dad explained it to me that it's called a kilt and that it's a secret what they wear underneath. Well, Bob dropped a box of poppies today and bent over to pick it up. Have you ever seen a Newfydoof blush? I didn't know where to look. Your secret's safe with me, Bob.

Me, dad and soldier Bob selling poppies

9th November 2013

That's it... Poppies all sold and am home again. Now it's time to get me bib washed and have a good brush and trim and early night ready for the parade. I'd say the same for Dad too, but it won't any diffyrence. He'll still look ... like Dad.

> Bob had asked Monty to join the parade around the town centre and to walk with him. Unfortunately, the band was right behind them and when the drums started up Monty decided he wanted to be somewhere else. We didn't want it to be a distraction, so we took him away out of earshot. We stood outside the church for the two-minute silence and when the bell chimed, he let out a howl which lasted for about thirty seconds. Iit was a very surreal and moving moment.

10th November 2013

I felt a bit bad today because I got scaredy when the banging started and didn't do the parade, but Dad said it didn't matter. He said the parade is for soldiers, old soldiers and mini-hooman cadetys. It was really nice to be asked but it's their day. He said the most important thing was collecting the money, and Soldier Bob said it's the best he's done in the seventeen ears he's been collecting there. He said it's 'cos I was there, and the money goes to help lots of hoomans. I feel better now... Looking forward to next ear already.

Yesterday I met Teddy up at Saneysberrys. She is a six-month-old girly Newfydoof and I fink I'm in lurv. She is gorgyuss. She has really pretty eyes and she was nice to me. I hope we meet again sometime.

11th November 2013

Just heard Dad saying the weather is looking OK for tomorrow. Great thinks I, we must be going somewhere special. Then he says must charge the camera up because I've got a few training videos to do... Nooooooo. Just when I thought he'd gone all soft and fuzzy.

Oh no! Dad says his broad bean is broke again and he's not happy. He says he is fed up with the virgin now and wants to go back to the sky. Not sure what he's talking about, it kinda sounds like he's going crazy – but what's new?

13th November 2013

Mum, Dad and Poobag all went out last night. Evidentiary they went to see someone called Ruby Murray. Never heard of her. Anyway, we got left in with the help and our kongs. Mine had some kibbley, some peanut butter, some yoghurt, some bandana and bungalow cheese. It was bootiful, but have you ever tried to eat your favourite food through a hole the size of a Spangle's brain? Next time you have fish and chips, Dad, I think you should try eating it out of a flask only using your tongue. There you go, that's your diet sorted.

> We thought that as Monty was now temporarily out of work, he might like to try carting. After all, allegedly he is a working breed.

15th November 2013

Dad has bought me a cart. Wow, thanks. You spend most days telling people I'm not a horse and then you want me to pull a cart. What's next, a nosebag and blinkers?

16th November 2013

It's a nice morning. I had brekkie and now I'm just lying here in the garden listening to the ducks and coots gently splashing around as they begin their early morning dabbling, looking for food. All I can think is if I could just get over that fence, how much trouble would they be in?

17th November 2013

Woke up this morning to find bits of fur on the carpet. I thought I was having a bad dream then I realised I'd had a haircut. Now, I know you hoomans are used to waking up after a night out experiencing similar things, but I'm a dog ... and in my own home... It's shocking!

18th November 2013

Just ruinated a hooman's day. We see these three lassie asbos who almost explode barking when they see us. They were walking down the road in their nice little pink coats when they spotted us. They went into yappy-drive and started doing pirrynets. Their hoomans decided to hide behind a lorry while me and Hippo Girl walked past 'cos, they were waking everyone up. Schoolboy error there, funny hoomans. They have teeny tiny legs and just carried on having a nervous breakdance while they watched us UNDER the lorry. It's a good thing you hoomans don't run this planet... Oh no, you do.

19th November 2013

I hate bin day. The hoomans line 'em all up down the street. You can't concentrate on your sniffing 'cos that sound of you whacking your head just puts you off. At least I didn't walk into a van door like somebody I know. Don't worry, your secret is safe with me, Cookie... Oops.

I have just had a dating request on Farcebook messenger from Julia... She seems nice enough though she doesn't appear to like cloths very much. Do you think I should tell her about the op? The other thing is, if I go on a date with her do you think head collar or not? And which bib should I wear?

20th November 2013

Now, I know it's not the done thing to watch a lady while she does the toilet thing, but Poppy just did seventeen circles before she did a wee. When she started doing number twos, I thought she was drilling for oil. With that amount of spinning she must be dizzy all day ... oh wait, she is. I don't know why I'm surprised really – after all, it is raining and she is a Spangle.

21 November 2013

Cookie went up to the learning zoo this morning. She hadn't been up for a while, so the mini- hoomans got lots of kisses. So sweet seeing them running off into the playground holding hands. It's not because they want to, it's just because they're stuck together ... bless.

25th November 2013

I know you hoomans don't like Mondays, but how else are we going to live in the manner that we've grown acostumed to if you don't get your lazy backsides out of bed and go and earn some money? PS. We're down to our last crate of treats. Order some more, Dad, there's a good serpant.

27th November 2013

Mum and Dad have been rushing round these last few days, like flies with bums painted blue. Dad had no time to listen to me funny stories and help me type, so I said, 'OK, you come up with something witty and amusing.' Guess what? Yes, that's the silence you've been hearing the last few days.

28th November 2013

When Dad took the Spangles out yesterday, Bailey ran straight into a metal gatepost 'cos: 1. He was sooo excited, and 2. Because he's stoopid. I heard Dad say that it may teach him to look where he's going. They just came back from their walk and Bailey walked into the patio door, which was closed. That'll be a no, then.

> Monty seemed to be perfect at charity work, so we decided to take him to a Christmas tree pull. Selling poppies for cuddles was one thing but what would he feel about more effort for a good cause?

29th November 2013

Tomorrow, if I get this right, I am getting my cart, putting a tree in it and taking it to a hooman's car. Then they give some money to someone called Charity. OK, I have a couple of questions. Do I get to do a wee up every tree? Second, why don't they just park a bit closer? Third, who is Charity and will they give her some treats? Seems fair, 'cos it's us doglets doing all the work here.

So if today is Black Friday, is tomorrow White and Black Saturday? If that's the case, I may go and hide somewhere on Brown Sunday.

1st December 2013

I was very excited yesterday when I was told, 'You are going somewhere really special.' Yeah? 'You're going to have a really fun day.' Yeah? 'You're going to meet a really special person.' Ooh, I can't wait. He is a big fat man with a red nose. Oh, is that all? I live with one of those.

CHAPTER 14
Monty Pulls At Last

As well as the charity work, Monty had been enrolled as a home checker. Sadly, a lot of Newfoundlands end up in rescue, so it's good to take one to a prospective new owner's home if applicants haven't experienced the breed up close.

If Monty comes to your house, you will certainly have an experience – and it will be very up close.

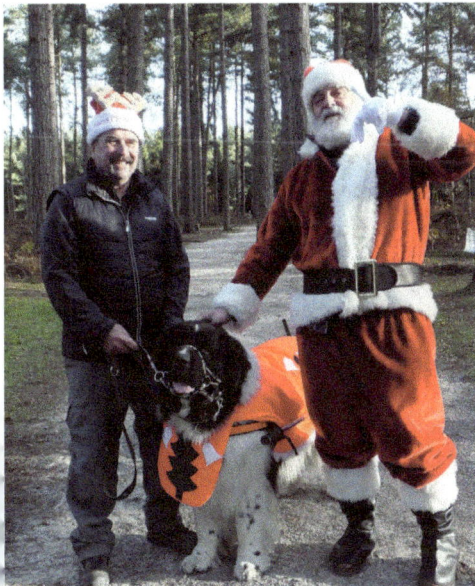

Santa meets a cwissymouse superstar

2nd December 2013

Busy week for me coming up. Next weekend I am doing some more pulling. Mum said I need to explain that to Dad 'cos he's never pulled anything in his life. I think that's another hooman joke.

In the week I am doing something called a home check. Dad says that's where people see me and if they can cope with me, they can cope with anything. I think that one might be an insult. Who knows what goes on in Dad's head?

3rd December 2013

OK, it's nearly Cwissymouse. I feel we went through this before at Hallyweener with Mick's messages (who is this Mick?). You spend all year scaring the mini-hoomans about not talking to the strangers and then you let – no you encourage – some big guy to come down the chimney and sneak into your kid's room to leave pressies! Not only that, but you leave him a drink for doing it. Do you realise how much you hoomans confuse us doglets? Where does that leave us for the canine system? What, we just let this one in – or is anyone OK as long as they dress up and bring some security gifts?

4th December 2013

Off to Yorkshire Pudding Land tomorrow, Sattyday and Sunday. Dad says he's there that often he may have to buy a flat cap, get a whippet and moan every time he has to spend money. Mum says he just needs the cap and the whippet.

5th December 2013

Be careful out there, all you Spangle owners. I'm worried this wind could turn them into lots of those little helicopter things that fall off the trees.

6th December 2013

That's it, Me and the Cookster have been confined to barracks while the hoomans put all the Cwissymouse decadent rations up. Mum said she wants me out the way cos I'm a big fat lump and I just get in the way... HELLO! Dad is still there. How does he get to stay?

Dad has just blinged me wheels ... he's pimped my ride ... he's ... he's ... stuck glittery things all over it. I'm gonna look camper than Liver Archies. Come on, Dad, all the guys are gonna laff at me this weekend. You can get beat up for this sort of stuff in Yorkshire Pudding Land, tha noors.

7th December 2013

Been to Sheffheeled today to do a bit of pulling. Didn't manage to pull either Maddie or Mia, two very sweet Newfydoof laydees, but give me time and they'll warm to me. We were doing a charity event for a mini-hooman hospice, which seems a really good cause. We was taking the mini-hoomans round the car park in our carts and taking people's food back to their car. It was good, got lots of treats I was allowed, and lots I weren't... Mini- hoomans holding doughnuts are like ducks who are sitting down. I'm sure I'll burn those callyrees off tomorrow.

9th December 2013

The car is fixed and we have wheels again. Dad says he's taking me and Cookie to the beach in the morning to make up for missing tree pulling on Sundleday. Me and Cookie on the beach? Uh oh, I am going to get more battered than a piece of Grimsby cod in a chippie. Nowhere to run or hide for this big fella on the Formby sands. Can we just go for a quiet walk? Dad ... DAD ... DAAAAADDDDDDD...

10ᵗʰ December 2013

Oh great. Just heard Cookie doing her best Winston
Churchill impersynation: 'I will fight him on the beaches...'
Great, can't wait for a nice gentle stroll along the sand ...
not. I may ban the use of cameras as I'd hate there to be
any record of me screaming.

11ᵗʰ December 2013

There are some people moved in down the road and they
have a Massteef. We've met and I'll be honest – it don't like
me. Now I have a theory. It's ugly and I'm – well, obviously
I'm not. It usually prowls around with a hooman man person
but tonight it was wiv a lady. It nearly dragged her across
the road to get to me. Dad said it's a good job there was no
cars coming. Me? I think it's a good job Kwasee-mowdo got
no further, 'cos I'd have had to remind him how his face got
all squashed up in the first place.

Alongside the Facebook posts, another thing kind
of just happened. Absolutely Barking is the world's
most incompetent dog trainer and was actually
very easy for me do. I am such a fool with my dogs
and they don't listen to me, so it made for some
entertaining videos (Life According to Monty Dogge,
YouTube). I'd like to say it was a spoof character but
really it was just me being me.

13ᵗʰ December 2013

Think we're having our picture taken today for the
Cwissymouse. Dad says he wants the five of us sitting

together quietly next to him, with our Cwissymouse hats on. An easy task if you're absolutely barking.

Don't tell Cookie, but Mum had an idea. She said in just over a week a big bloke dressed in a red suit with a long white beard is going to sneak into the house. Her idea is that maybe Absolutely Barking should do some training with her, so she's used to him when he gets here. This can only end one way, methinks. Maybe he'll forget about the group photo... I can only hope.

14th December 2013

Tomorrow we are trying to get over to the forest to help pull the Cwissymouse trees. Dad says the car is fixed and he didn't do it himself so it should be OK. Mum isn't coming 'cos she has something called a 'works do'. Dad says it's where Mum goes with her fiends, drinks lots, eats lots, dances lots, then falls over and snores lots... Pretty normal day for her, then.

Dad's in party mood. He's just singing along with 'When the going gets tough, the tough get going'. He said, 'Someone once said I sound like Billy Ocean.' We think he misheard them. They said, 'Wish you'd drown in an ocean.' Simple mistake, really.

15th December 2013

That's it, up early, had me brekkie. Done numbers one to two and now ready for me trip to Yorkshire Pudding Land. Cart is packed, tyre pressures done and got me Cwissymouse coat and bib packed. Just need the hooman servyants to get me there on time and I'm ready for work. DAD, don't forget treats . No, not for you, stooped. Being with me all day is your treat.

It's fair to say Monty was a success at Christmas-tree pulling. Despite his laziness, most of the time he seemed to really enjoy it and of course he loved the attention.

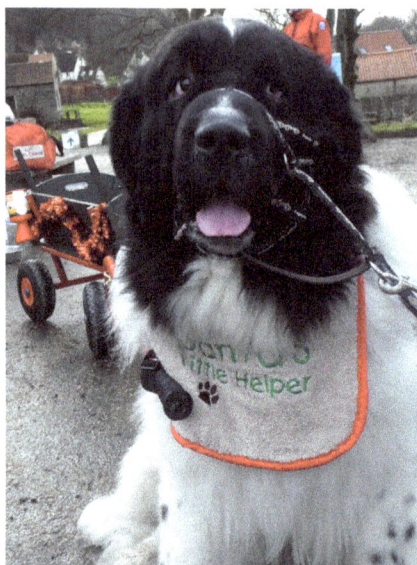

Monty waiting for his next customer

Have you seen the size of this tree?

16th December 2013

Just realised it's the morning. The last thing I remember was getting out of the car, having a wash and eating tea. Then ... nothing. I must have been really tired last night. I'm not sure whether it was all that tree pulling or listening to Dad talk for two-and-a-half hours in the car coming back. It's enough to send anyone off for the night.

17th December 2013

I was so looking forward to watching Cwissymouse films last night then Dad went out. That's OK because Mum's still here. Then she goes out too. OK, so what are me options? Cookie? The Spangles? Me stag bone? A night with me stag bone it is, then.

18th December 2013

Mum and Dad have been writing the Cwissymouse cards tonight. I had a little peek... I can't believe it – there's a Spangle on the front! I feel betrayed. How can that cheer people up over the festering season? Happy Cwissymouse, hope your ears don't drag in your gravy? Come on hoomans ... you cannot be serious.

19th December 2013

Dad is out again tonight, so he said we can't watch Cwissymouse films again, but after tonight he'll be in, so that's OK then. He said that when you've been good at Cwissymouse, good things happen to you, but if you've been really norty you have bad things happen to you.

Well, tonight he had to go and watch Sheffield Tuesday play Wigwam Not-very-athletic. You can guess how he's been this year, can't you?

20th December 2013

Out on our walk this morning, Dad was commenting how
I had changed and hadn't barked at the deckyrations in
the hoomans' front gardens this year. Well, as you know
my favvyreet hobby is proving him wrong, so I gave some
Monty chat to an eight-foot snowman. The hoomans in the
house fort it was funny. Dad just sighed and shook his head
... he does that a lot these days.

21st December 2013

Life's been a bit quiet this week. The hoomans have been
getting ready for the Cwissymouse by visiting everyone,
and today they go to Brummy-jum to see Nanny Cuckoo.
Tomorrow, though, I am going to a guarding centre called
Fart-on-Grange. I've been before. Coachloads of old ladies
turn up and do I get some fusses? The only thing is we
have to go through the 'Ah he's lovely, what's his name?'
'Monty...' 'Minty?' 'No Monnntttyyy' 'Hello, Marty, you're a
good boy, aren't you?'

Went to Fart-on-Grange today and met me two fwends,
Jude Brown Mitchell and Helen Hudson, who came to see me.
They pretended to Dad that they were the silly hoomans
who ask the stoopid questions about Newfydoofs, like what
make is it? They totally fooled him, even when they called
me Minty. It's nice when other people see what I have to
live with. Stoo...piddd.

22nd December 2013

I heard Mum and Dad talking last night. Evidentiary, Santa
is coming to our house a day early. Dad says Cookie will go
crazy when a stranger sneaks in, in the middle of the night
dressed in a red suit and big white beard. His answer to

that is to do some training with her on Cwissymouse Eve so she's totally calm... That sounds like a great idea. I'll bring the popcorn.

(Video can be found here. https://youtu.be/DwAO1IAu9AQ)

I'm going on a home check tomorrow with guess who. This is to check that someone wanting a dog is suitable and has the right home to bring the dog into, right? Well, I have two obseyvations on that. Firstly, did they check Dad out before he got me? And if they did, how did he ever pass? Can I get a recount and if not, can I sue? Secondly, how do people let him into their homes. We wouldn't let him in here if he didn't have a key.

23rd December 2013

Well, did me home check today and it was in Blackbum. It's a bit like wigwam but on a hill. I think I've got this home check stuff right. I have to be like the sort of doggie they may get. It could be norty, knocking stuff all over the place. It could have bad manners. It could eat their letters. It could be a hooligan, jumping around on the couch and chasing the cat... Yep got it ... Monty Dogge home-checker extraordinaire... NEXT.

CHAPTER 15
Me Rise To Stardom

25th December 2013

A Merry Cwissymouse to everyone, although I can't really see the point. OK, you're good all year ... yep. You write your letter to Santa ... yep. You tell him what you really, really, really want ... yep. You send him the letter by recorded elf mail ... yep. You go to sleep early ... yep.

I've done everything right but I woke up this morning, crept into the other room and the Spangles are still here, so what's the point? Oh well, try again next year.

MERRY CWISSYMOUSE EVERYONE ... and the Spangles.

Make a wish

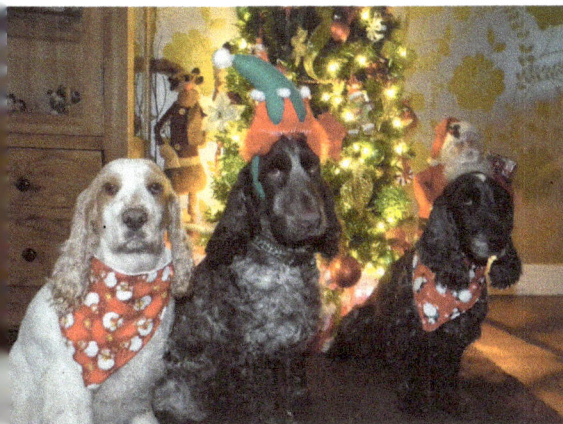

Nope, still there.

27th December 2013

This is one for my doglet fwends – please don't let the two-egged ones read this.

You may be unhappy about the pressies you got. You may be fed up seeing the upright walking ones eating, drinking and being too merry. But remember ... hoomans are for life, not just for Cwissymouse. So try to be patient and start with their training again as soon as they're sober.

I think in my case that could be some time.

28th December 2013

There seems to be a lot of party food left and not much coming my way. Cwissymouse has gone now, so maybe it's time to start eating sensibly again and ditch some of them sossygee rolls and biccies. Just to let you know, I'm always here to help.

1st December 2013

I have been a bit norty lately and have been grumpy with a few dogs on our walks. I can't help it because they say stuff under their breath that you hoomans can't hear like

'Here comes that massive one with his hooge dog' and 'Is it me, or is it Friesian around here?' Come on, what would you do? I'm only canine.

So we're back in training to improve my 'attitude' with other doggies. Leave, leave, leave. Good boy. OK, that seems easy enough. But that's a hooman schoolboy error, Dad; you forgot to say that about the bus. Ha-ha, I lurv chasing buses. The training continues.

Happy New Year to fellow Newfydoofs, other doglets (including Spangles), hoomans and any other variety (Dad).

Ha-ha. Love you really.

As we said goodbye to 2013, Monty was fast approaching his third birthday. He had calmed down and become a well-socialised dog, but he still kept us on our toes. With his new partner in crime, the incredibly bouncy two-year-old Cookie, we certainly knew we lived with giant dogs.

Not to be outdone, Molly, Poppy and Bailey kept us amused with their antics and there were plenty more stories to come...

See you next time, when Monty unexpectedly becomes a blogger at Crufts, gets crowned the self-titled Poet Newfiette and continues to share his thoughts on living in Wigwam with his ever-so-slightly dysfunctional family.

Until then we'll leave you with a few words from the dog himself...

Me rise to stardom by Monty Dogge

When I was little I was very, very bad.
The hoomans despaired of the puppy they had.
I'd chew and I'd bite and break lots of stuff
Till Dad said one day that enough was enough.

'Monty, my boy, please try and be good.
You have to do something to earn all this food.'
I fort long and hard about the skills that I had.
I know – I'll make hoomans larf and I'll tell them about Dad.

I could tell all the stories of the things that we do,
Watching him dodge the traffic to pick up me poo.
Tell how he gets grumpy and goes red in the face
When me and the heffalump drag him all over the place

So I went on to Farcebook and got me a page,
Cos I know this unsocial media stuff is all the rage.
I just needed a goatwriter 'cos typing was tough –
Newfydoof paws ain't too good with that stuff.

So me hooman buffoon (or Dad, as we call him)
Was given the job of serving my whim.
I started telling all my tails and stories
Hoping you hoomans would want to read more(ies).

I started to get lots of likes on me posts
And comments about the fings you liked the mosts.
The number of fwends I had just kept on growing
So me stories kept coming – I couldn't be slowing.

I was even allowed to go to a show
Where all the posh dogs and their hooman slaves go.
This was Crufts; I dreamt I would win
But Dad said, 'You'll be lucky if they just let you in.'

There were Spangle tails that were easy to explain
'Cos they're either acting stoopid or being a pain.
And Emma became a hooman who got renamed Poobag –
not the sort of fame to make someone brag.

And last but not least, there's the hooge heffalump
Whose favourite activity is to make Dad a chump.
He showed how to train her and danced with her too
All on a video for peoples to view.

My rise to stardom has been very fast
And has made up for my norty Newfy past.
But me hoomans sometimes need a memory jog
So I go back to being cheeky ... the old Monty Dogge...

Newfydoof Dictionary

We hope you are now fluent in Newfydoof, but if you're still not totally sure here's some help.

Newfydoof	Newfoundland
Wigwam	Wigan
Hooman	Human
Mini-Hooman	Child
Learning Zoo	School
Cockeyed Spangle	Cocker Spaniel
Vetandhairyman	Veterinarian
Burnt knees mounting dog	Bernese Mountain Dog
Snack Rustle	Jack Russell
Cwissymouse	Christmas
Lassie Asbo	Lhasa Apso
Bored old collie	Border Collie
Snotwhiler	Rottweiler
Farcebook	Facebook
Ringdaft	Ring Craft

Guys dog	Guide dog
Keysound	Keeshond
Booby day in flanders	Bouvier des Flandres
Shitty-Zoo	Shih Tzu
Camel Tarred	Camouflaged
Cartoon Ourness	Carting harness
Myflection	My reflection
Snawtzer	Schnauzer
Special lips	Specialist
Hippo condriate	Hypochondriac
Dog that's bored now	Dog de Bordeaux
Micks Messages	Mixed messages
Hilary arse	Hilarious

Acknowledgments

This story has been such a wonderful adventure that I can't finish without paying tribute to those who have made it possible.

Firstly, to all of you that started as followers and fans but have become friends. Without your amazing support and generosity none of this would ever have happened. You have liked, shared and joined in with our tales. You have bought the books and donated to the charity appeals over and over again. Thank you. This is truly your story too.

Whilst it would be lovely to thank everyone individually, it just isn't possible. I would, however like to make a few special mentions in each of this series of books.

Firstly, to Auntie Vivian McPhee for dressing Monty and Cookie so beautifully with her fabulous bibs and never taking a penny, instead just asking for a donation to charity.

To Nick Overmire for writing the Pandacow song, which is stuck in everyone's heads forever, and to Megan Turner for her wonderful performance.

To Wullie and Yvonne Burt for their fantastic hospitality during all our visits to Scottyland, and to Patty Jens Balodis for her amazing fundraising to donate our books to children in Baltimore and California.

A massive thank you to Zoe Saunders (Whimsicolour Art) who has brought Monty's stories to life with her beautiful illustrations and is always a pleasure to work with.

Also big thanks to Helen Overmire, not only for the cover photo but the fantastic pictures of Monty that she took and we still use almost daily. You are a real talent. Thank you.

To our wonderful 'vetandhairyman' Luc Van Dijck and the amazing staff at the surgery. They always go that extra mile to care for all of our dogs. Thank you for your compassion and professionalism.

As always, I must give a huge thanks to our publisher 2QT who are wonderful folk to work with. Catherine is a constant source of support and information and a superb sounding board for authors. Karen, our editor, finds that perfect balance between making everything read correctly while keeping the story true. I think she is also the first editor in the world to have edited a book in Newfydoof – and what a job she's done. Thanks, Karen. A big shout out to Dale for putting everything together and making the process seamless.

And last, but definitely not least, my family. To Dawn, a huge thanks for putting up with me all these years. You are my biggest critic and biggest supporter and certainly never sugarcoat anything. I do appreciate it – not always at the time, but I do. Thanks. I love you loads.

To my own mini-hoomans and their partners who are always a constant source of support and encouragement, a massive thank you to Emma, Sam, Becky, Tina, and Gary. I love you.

More titles from the author

Check out this lovely series of childrens books starring Monty and the gang.

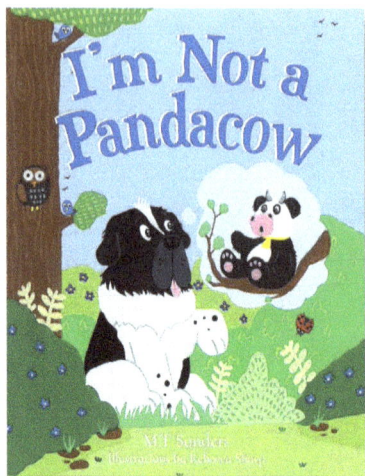

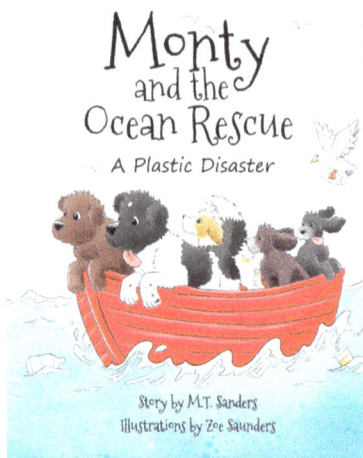

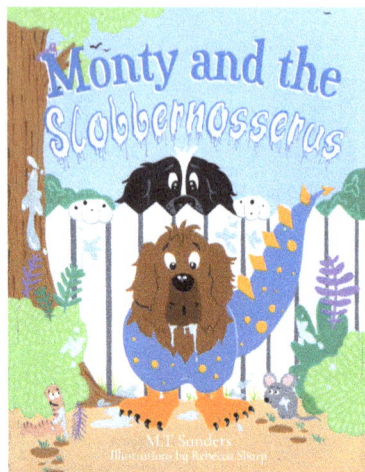

Monty
and the
Land of the
DINODOGS

Story by M.T. Sanders
Illustrations by Zoe Saunders

Monty and Friends
African Adventure
The Mission to Save Kaluwa

Story by M.T. Sanders
Illustrations by Zoe Saunders

Monty
and the
Poppit Dragon

Story by M.T. Sanders
Illustrations by Zoe Saunders

Monty
and friends
save
Christmas

Story by M.T. Sanders
Illustrations by Zoe Saunders

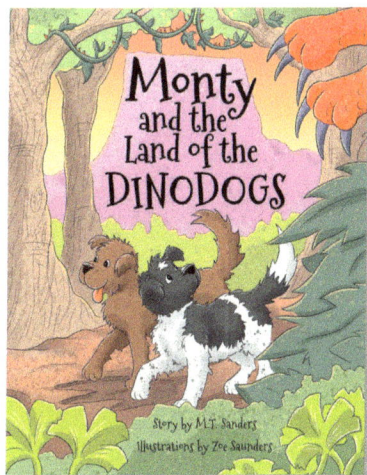

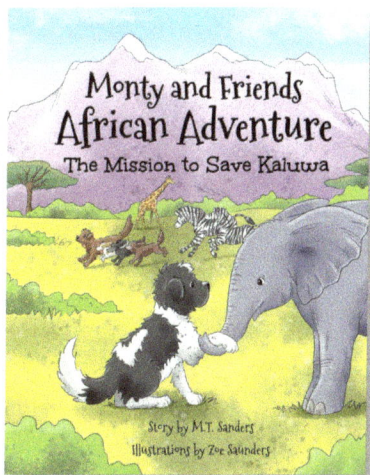

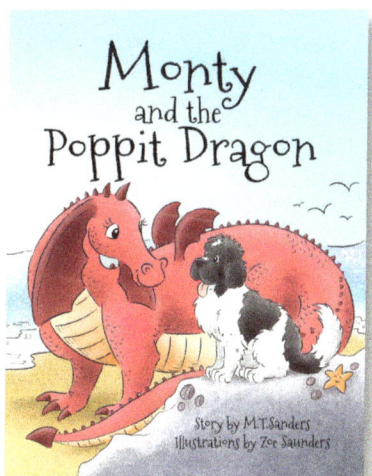

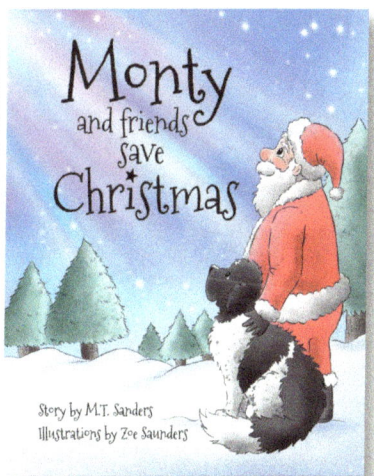

https://montydogge.com/our-books

Lightning Source UK Ltd.
Milton Keynes UK
UKHW020315160821
388814UK00008B/148